A METHODIST REQUIEM

Words of Hope and Resurrection
for the Church

WILLIAM B. LAWRENCE

A Methodist Requiem: Words of Hope and Resurrection for the Church

The General Board of Higher Education and Ministry leads and serves The United Methodist Church in the recruitment, preparation, nurture, education, and support of Christian leaders— lay and clergy—for the work of making disciples of Jesus Christ for the transformation of the world. Its vision is that a new generation of Christian leaders will commit boldly to Jesus Christ and be characterized by intellectual excellence, moral integrity, spiritual courage, and holiness of heart and life. The General Board of Higher Education and Ministry of The United Methodist Church serves as an advocate for the intellectual life of the church. The Board's mission embodies the Wesleyan tradition of commitment to the education of laypersons and ordained persons by providing access to higher education for all persons.

Wesley's Foundery Books is named for the abandoned foundery that early followers of John Wesley transformed into a church, which became the cradle of London's Methodist movement.

A Methodist Requiem: Words of Hope and Resurrection for the Church

Copyright 2018 by Wesley's Foundery Books.

Wesley's Foundery Books is an imprint of the General Board of Higher Education and Ministry, The United Methodist Church. All rights reserved.

Notes refer to 1972, 1996, 2008, 2012, and 2016 editions of *The Book of Discipline of The United Methodist Church* (Nashville: The United Methodist Publishing House).

All web addresses were correct and operational at the time of publication.

ISBN 978-0-938162-46-9

18 19 20 21 22 23 24 25 26 27—10 9 8 7 6 5 4 3 2 1
Manufactured in the United States of America

HIGHER EDUCATION & MINISTRY
General Board of Higher Education and Ministry
THE UNITED METHODIST CHURCH

Hear my prayer:

To you shall all flesh come;
Eternal rest grant unto them, O Lord,
And let perpetual light shine upon them.

Introit from *Requiem*

CONTENTS

PROLOGUE

REQUIEM AS A METHOD OF PRAYER AND HOPE

For Christians, the word *requiem* has a special meaning as a voice of hope. It is our witness to the promise of resurrection and the power of life, surpassing even death.

Requiem is a rite[1] that links prayers of praise and language of lament with petitions for the dead—that the dead will be raised and that they will find eternal rest among the saints. Christians may use Requiem at funerals and on All Saints Day. And it is not just an order of texts with words of hope. Requiem has beguiled hundreds of composers to create nearly two thousand works to play and sing.

A choir may sing one of these compositions during Holy Week, when the church is in the midst of contemplating the suffering and death of Jesus. But Requiem is not an elegy about Christ's crucifixion. Rather, it is an order of prayer that accepts the Lord's redemptive sacrifice, trusts his resurrection, and finds hope for the grieving and the dead. It affirms our belief that we will, by God's grace, enter into the realm of "eternal rest" (in the opening words of introit) and "into paradise" (in the closing words of benediction).

In secular usage, the word *requiem* often refers to a tragic end. *Requiem for a Heavyweight* is Rod Serling's script about the hopeless outcome of a life in professional boxing. *Requiem for the American Dream* conveys Noam Chomsky's grim sense that the American experiment—with government by representative democracy and with equitable economic opportunity for all—is coming to an end.

But, as a Christian witness, Requiem expresses everlasting hope that

---

1   Within the liturgical format of Requiem, there are variations in the number, order, and verbal content of the texts. Composers have made adaptations as well. The citations in this book for Requiem texts follow an English translation of the pattern of the Latin liturgy for the Requiem Mass in the Western church. Gabriel Fauré, who composed and revised his own version of Requiem, provided one example of this form. And his version was the result of a creative process that lasted several years and that remains a matter of study. The format of the Fauré Requiem is a significant influence upon the pattern adapted for this book, though some of its theological emphases are not consistent with the Wesleyan tradition.

draws from the eternal promises of God. It applies God's love to those whose deaths we mourn. And it inspires our trust in God's care for the church, for the institutions that nurture our faith, and for the mission on which we are sent as believers. It is for us and for our salvation.

In this spirit, I present the following pages as *A Methodist Requiem*. Its purpose is not to grieve a loss but to claim a promise. My hope for the church is that we remain unshaken by the challenges we face. In fact, my hope is strengthened by the mission to which God has called us in the world. It is the foundation on which our faith is built. In too many places, too many people hear only the sounds of despair and death. But the crucified and risen Lord has summoned us and sent us to proclaim the truth of life. Our hope is built on nothing less.

So we craft the message in words of hope. We celebrate the message in the music of resurrection. We believe in the process of salvation by God's grace. We trust that this process is guiding us toward a goal where God's love perfectly prevails.

The mission of Methodism will endure. We will continue to sing of love divine, all loves excelling. And we will be inspired to hope that this life will offer all of God's children abundant tastes of eternal joy along our journey toward paradise.

PART ONE

THE RHETORIC OF FAITH

King of majesty tremendous,
Who does free salvation send us,
Font of pity, then befriend us!

Think, kind Jesus! My salvation
Caused thy wondrous incarnation.
Leave me not to reprobation.

Dies Irae (*Day of Wrath*) from *Requiem*

FINDING THE WORDS

In one biblical account, a woman named Mary Magdalene visited the tomb early on the first day of the week, while it was still dark. She felt she was in the dark too.

> She ran and went to Simon Peter and the other disciple, the one whom Jesus loved, and said to them, "They have taken the Lord out of the tomb, and we do not know where they have laid him." (John 20:2)

> Mary stood weeping outside the tomb. . . . and she saw two angels in white, sitting where the body of Jesus had been lying. . . . She said to them, "They have taken away my Lord, and I do not know where they have laid him." (John 20:11–13)

> Supposing him to be the gardener, she said to him, "Sir, if you have carried him away, tell me where you have laid him, and I will take him away." (John 20:15)

In another biblical account, a group of women visited the tomb at dawn. They had prepared to pay respects to one who was sealed in death. They were not prepared for life.

> On the sabbath they rested according to the commandment. But on the first day of the week, at early dawn, they came to the tomb, taking the spices that they had prepared. . . . they did not find the body. While they were perplexed about this, suddenly two men in dazzling clothes stood beside them. . . . "Why do you look for the living among the dead?" (Luke 23:56–24:5)

In yet another Biblical witness, a reassuring voice encourages endurance and inspires persistence among the living.

> Here is a call for the endurance of the saints, those who keep the commandments of God and hold fast to the faith of Jesus. And I heard a voice from heaven saying, "Write this: Blessed are the dead who from now on die in the Lord." "Yes," says the Spirit, "they will rest from their labors, for their deeds follow them." (Revelation 14:12–13)

MATTERS OF DEATH AND LIFE

Methodism has been a marvelous movement in mission for Jesus Christ across nearly three hundred years of Christian history. It began as a student group committed to study and service. It blossomed with spiritual renewal inside the Anglican Church. And it became a denomination when the United States was becoming a constitutional nation.

Methodism has broadened in three centuries to every inhabited continent on earth. It has built institutions to heal the unhealthy, research the unknown, teach the unlearned, nourish the unfed, reach the unsaved, and befriend the unloved. It has lifted the lost from despair, broken the bonds of slavery, braced addicts for freedom from dependence, based ministers in communities as its agents of transformation, and blessed all of God's people with good news that death is defeated by life. It is both pious practice and public power.

Methodism has contributed mightily to the history of Christianity. It is a viable presence as a religious minority in lands where other religions dominate. It has been a vital presence in lands where religion has been driven underground by political regimes. It offers a profound presence where sentimentality is sold as a substitute for spirituality.

In every hemisphere, the Methodist mission has transformed private souls and public systems. In places, Methodism has made a major difference. Some historians and social scientists have looked at the violent political upheaval of the French Revolution and concluded that Methodism offered the means of grace that met the grievances of the oppressed social classes. So, on another side of the English Channel, the French Revolution had no analogue in England, these scholars argue. There was much death on the continent during the late 1700s. There was news of life where the Methodist mission took hold.

Methodism has been versatile and adaptable in its mission, so it could take root in many different kinds of settings and situations. One major factor is that the Methodists' mission is a connection—a distinctive unity expressed in forms of diversity. Through this connectional church system, "God has been steadily at work, both within and despite human plans, decisions, and actions," says United Methodism's Committee on Faith and Order.[1]

As a result, Methodism has found ways to witness all over the planet, especially during recent decades. It lasted in Cuba for generations while rule was imposed by Castro and while isolation was attempted by the United

---

1   *Wonder, Love, and Praise: Sharing a Vision of the Church*, Committee on Faith and Order, The United Methodist Church, for the Council of Bishops of The United Methodist Church in 2017, lines 260–61.

States. Methodism discovered the means to become a voice for the poor in Colombia while the country was being ravaged by militarism and drug wars. It seized space at the intersection of theological disputes in Costa Rica, where voices of conservative and liberationist perspectives engaged in debates. It contributed to creating post-colonial freedom in Malaysia and Singapore, finding different forms for Methodism to gain a multiethnic identity in these Asian lands. It has grown more than anyone could have imagined in sub-Saharan Africa, where its faithfulness has become a source of hope.

The world applauded when Nelson Mandela emerged from the prison that had confined him for twenty-seven years. He had kept his dignity, identity, integrity, and hope intact for more than a generation. While the cruelty and corruption of the apartheid system ruled his homeland and restricted him to exile on an island away from home, he remained true to the values and virtues that he said Methodism had nurtured in him. When he was finally free, he took those principles to the presidency of South Africa. His new nation then began a process of truth and reconciliation, so South Africans could confess the evils of apartheid while moving beyond its destructive systems.

The world also noted when a new nation emerged from an oppressive colonial era in Rhodesia. However, under its independent name, Zimbabwe has now been oppressed for nearly forty years by its post-colonial president. So Methodism has been learning how to be a voice of prophecy under the tyrannical Mugabe regime. One United Methodist minister reported that the authorities seized her and sent her to a tribunal after some spies heard her Sunday sermon and perceived it to have been critical of the government. The tribunal demanded that she provide them with a report on her sermon. She said to the agents of government, "I do not give reports on sermons. I preach them." So she stood there before the tribunal and preached the same sermon again. After she concluded, they deliberated briefly. And they let her go.[2] Like so many in the land of Zimbabwe under Mugabe, she was facing the prospect of death. She confronted it with the gospel of life.

The message of Methodism has always been a matter of death and

---

2   The Rev. Dr. Christinah Kwaramba shared her account of this incident in a conversation with the author.

life. Its mission has delivered the gospel to whatever kills hope, whatever kills happiness, whatever kills progress, whatever kills fairness, whatever kills children's laughter, whatever kills joy, whatever kills freedom, whatever kills reason, and whatever just plain kills.

John Wesley founded Methodism to bring a renewal of life into the established Church of England. The forerunners of its creation as a denomination in North America took its mission of life to scattered small villages, squalid urban settings, and solitary spots on the frontier. Those who formed the mission into a Methodist Episcopal Church of the United States of America devised methods for leading small groups, conducting camp revivals, deploying itinerant preachers, and educating future leaders. They were determined to teach the doctrines of Wesleyan theology, form disciples in the Wesleyan tradition, and dismantle evil systems such as slavery that opposed the Wesleyan spirit.

John Wesley said in 1744 at his first conference of preachers that the mission of Methodism was to "reform the nation and more particularly the church . . . spreading scriptural holiness."[3] In 1784, in their founding conference, North American Methodists declared that the mission was "to reform the continent and spread scriptural holiness over these lands."[4] So the mission of Methodism clearly addresses the social systems in the world as well as the spiritual souls of the world. That means preaching, teaching, incorporating, and institutionalizing the good news in Jesus Christ through whom God has given us a victory over sin and death. In short, for individuals and for society, it is a message of death and life.

It is not unusual to hear extreme circumstances described as matters "of life and death." Ironically, it has been said in the United States and in Europe about football: "It's not a matter of life and death. It's way more important than that!"

But a much more appropriate form of the phrase for Christians, including those of us who belong to the Methodist tradition founded by

---

3   According to *The 'Large' Minutes*, this was on or about June 28, 1744. *The Works of John Wesley: The Methodist Societies, The Minutes of Conferences*, vol. 10, ed. Henry D. Rack (Nashville: Abingdon Press, 2011), 845.

4   Russell E. Richey, "United Methodist Doctrine and Teaching on the Nature, Mission and Faithfulness of the Church: A Resource Paper from The UMC Committee on Faith and Order," May 3, 2013, p. 18.

John Wesley, is that our faith is *a matter of death and life.*" The rhetoric of Christianity does not end with a word about death, because we proclaim that death has been overcome. We believe that death is not the final force.

"Love is strong as death," according to a poet in the Old Testament.[5] "Hope is stronger than death," says a note attached to a 911 memorial.[6] "As all die in Adam, so all will be made alive in Christ,"[7] the apostle Paul wrote. We move from death to life.

When the first followers of the faith began sharing the gospel, they focused upon Jesus' death on the cross and his life as the Risen One. Perhaps the first Christian sermon was one delivered "with fear and great joy" that Jesus, who had died, was raised to life.[8] Christianity is a matter of death and life. But fear of death still haunts the human spirit.

The movie *Moonstruck* won three academy awards, including Oscars for best actress (Cher), best supporting actress (Olympia Dukakis), and best original screenplay (John Patrick Shanley). It has one of the finest concluding scenes ever in a film, as the main characters gather for breakfast in a kitchen and resolve the conflicts in the story. It also addresses a perplexing moral question, which is woven into the plot.

Dukakis's character presses people for an answer to her question, "Why do men chase women?" It is not an abstract query. Her husband is unfaithful. In a church where she has gone to pray, she tells their daughter, played by Cher, "Cosmo is cheating on me." Eventually, she puts the question to her soon-to-be son-in-law, played by Danny Aiello. "But why would a man need more than one woman?" she asks.

"I don't know," he replies. "Maybe because he fears death."

"That's it!" she says. "Thank you for answering my question!"[9]

The fear of death has been used to explain a lot of things, including philandering. Fear of death may motivate someone to accumulate more wealth than could possibly be spent during a typical lifetime, in a fantasy

---

5   Song of Solomon 8:6.

6   Tony Mussari, "Shanksville: Where Hope is Stronger than Death," http://www.faceofamerica
wps.com/news/shanksville-where-hope-is-stronger-than-death/.

7   1 Corinthians 15:22.

8   Matthew 28:8.

9   *Moonstruck* (1987) was written by John Patrick Shanley and directed by Norman Jewison.

that buying more could delay the end. Or fear of death might motivate someone to accumulate great power as a means to feel secure against every possible threat, even mortality. And fear of death might motivate someone to become religious, in an effort to quell the anxiety. "Some say that religion is, at base, a mechanism to handle the human response to mortality and loss," wrote Patricia J. Williams in a review of a posthumous memoir by the late Coretta Scott King.[10] But Mrs. King's pursuit of justice outpaced any fear. Faith is more than fear.

Nevertheless, Christianity is a religion that addresses the fear of death. The faith takes death seriously, and it does not offer any refuge from death. Instead, the power of Christianity is its direct confrontation with death and its claim of victory over death.

The earliest Christians built their beliefs around the story of a weekend in the city of Jerusalem. A teacher, called Jesus of Nazareth, was executed by an occupying force of the Roman imperial government on a Friday. Then he was proclaimed as raised from the dead on a third day, Sunday.

Plenty of people—including many Christians—have been skeptical about claims that the dead body of Jesus was restored physically to life. But all Christians trust that a mysterious and transcendent hope is built around the life of Jesus. With that assurance, Christians confront death-dealing systems—from ignorance to injustice, from disease to despair. Christians create methods and institutions in efforts to overcome such systems.

Christians' rituals, notably the sacraments of Baptism and Holy Communion, are sacred celebrations of victory over death. Christians' creeds include affirmations of belief in the death and resurrection of Jesus. Christians' worship patterns focus on Sunday, the first day of the week, since it was the day of Jesus' resurrection. Christians' funeral rites express the conviction that death is not the last word. Christians' music, architecture, and art take forms that point beyond the boundary of death. Christians celebrate martyrs, who sacrificed themselves as witnesses to the faith at the point of death so that others might find joy and peace in life. Christians name their churches and their children for such saints. Christians construct calendars in cycles that feature the days of Jesus' birth, death, and resurrection on

10   Patricia J. Williams, "Mrs. King and Coretta," review of *My Life, My Love, My Legacy* (New York: Henry Holt & Company, 2017), *New York Times Magazine*, January 15, 2017, p 9.

Easter—including the consequences of his resurrection in his living presence in the life of the church through the Holy Spirit.

Easter, according to one study[11] that confirms the experiences of nearly every pastor, is the biggest day in the church year. Crowds at worship are larger than on any other Sunday. Churches add services to the schedule or move to larger facilities—like basketball arenas or football stadiums—to find sufficient room for everyone. Musicians offer their best, brightest, and brassiest ways to celebrate with choruses of "Hallelujah!"

On Easter, Christian communities honor their most distinctive and most treasured traditions, like the Orthodox whose hours-long Easter Vigil begins in deep dark silence until a single candle light emerges. Then the first words are spoken in Greek as the priest says, *"Christos Aneste!"* ("Christ Is Risen!"), and light is passed from one person to another by sharing the fire from the tips of tapers until the whole church is bathed in beautiful light.

Easter is the church's day of greatest joy. Christmas is splendid, of course, and there is an enormous confluence of sacred and secular practices that create the culture of Christmas. But, with some small exceptions (like Easter candy, hunting for decorated eggs, or singing "Easter Parade" from the 1948 film of the same name), Easter belongs to the church. And, on Easter, the church abounds in joy. Hymns ecstatically echo the news that "Christ the Lord Is Risen Today" and implore believers to sing in triumph, *"Cristo vive, fuera el llanto, los lamentos y el pesar!"*[12] Symbols tend to be trumpeting tributes, like the lilies that open wide in white and gold and green or the hyacinths that exude sweet aromas like incense that spreads through the worship space so everything that breathes can praise the Lord.[13]

Easter is Christianity's definitive day. In the earliest era of the faith, Christians chose the first day of the week as their principal occasion for worship because, as they shared the story, it was "early in the morning on the first day of the week" that the news of Christ's resurrection broke upon the

---

11   "Mother's Day Church Attendance Third Among Holidays" (LifeWayResearch.com, May 11, 2012).

12   "Christ is risen, Christ is living, dry your tears, be unafraid!" *The United Methodist Hymnal* (Nashville: The United Methodist Publishing House, 1989), 302 and 313. (English translation in the hymnal.)

13   Psalm 150:6.

world. Each Sunday became a "little Easter" for the early church and for Christians in the millennia thereafter.

Easter is a day when some churches choose to celebrate a sacrament of initiation. The defining event for a believer to enter fully into the life of the church is baptism. For followers of Christ, it is not a sign of cleansing or renewal but a symbol of entry into the death and resurrection of Jesus Christ.

Christian baptism is not just a sign of repentance, as it was for John the Baptist. Rather, Christian baptism is a symbol of death and life. That is most obvious when the ritual involves complete immersion.

One can be baptized by immersion in different places: in an interior pool, like the ones commonly found in Baptist churches; in a small font, like the ones where infants are immersed in Orthodox liturgies; in a large font, like the ones that are found increasingly in Catholic churches; or in a river, stream, pond, lake, or ocean, where baptisms are occasionally practiced by Protestants. Immersion into the waters of baptism can be, both visibly for worshiping communities and experientially for one being baptized, a symbolic plunge into the death of Christ from which one then is lifted in resurrection with Christ.

A baptized Christian is a child of Easter, a member of the community of the resurrection, with a new family of sisters and brothers in a communion of saints. Indeed, the baptized one has a new life and a new identity. In ancient practice, in fact, a newly baptized person received a Christian name and publicly wore a new garment that defined her or his new identity as a believer grafted into the resurrected life of Christ.

Easter expresses the biblical foundation of our faith. The witness in Scripture is unequivocal. All four Gospels testify to the message that Christ has been raised from the dead—even the Gospel of Mark, whose original ending says that the first persons to hear news of the resurrection on the first Easter were dumbstruck, "for terror and amazement had seized them."[14] The message of Paul is unambiguous: "in fact Christ has been raised from the dead."[15] And, besides the pages of the New Testament, where the witness to the resurrection is consistent, ancient prophecies echo: that "the LORD of hosts . . . will swallow up death forever";[16] and that the breath of the Lord came to

---

14   Mark 16:8.

15   1 Corinthians 15:20.

16   Isaiah 25:6, 8.

the bones of those who had died, "and they lived, and stood on their feet, a vast multitude."[17]

Easter is the core of Christianity's creedal statements of faith that unite believers. The Nicene Creed and the Apostles' Creed both say of Jesus Christ, "on the third day, he rose." While individuals may hold a variety of views about interpreting this article of the faith, and while theologians through the centuries have debated the meaning of that tenet in our teaching, Christians' official statements of belief have always asserted it.

Easter is the center of the story that Christians share. It acknowledges that we do indeed see our religion as a response to the fear of death. However, we do not cower in the face of it or feel defeated by the force of it. In the gospel of Jesus, we confront it. We overcome it. We tell the story of the death and life of Jesus. We proclaim that God's Holy Spirit lives and dwells with us in the church of Jesus Christ—that we are the people of the resurrection.

But Easter is not an isolated event. The resurrection of Jesus is inseparable from the death of Jesus. To say the Lord has risen is to say the Lord has died.

It was actually Jesus' death that perplexed some of the earliest Christians. Their debates dealt with the curiosity about whether Jesus was truly a human being who really died. Was he, instead, just a phantom or a feeling? Was he, perhaps, an image or an idea? Was he merely a memorably good teacher to whom followers attached some magic and mystery and myth, making him more of a conceptual principle than a person of flesh and blood?

With determination, Christians said No! to such notions. Jesus not only lived, but he also died. Jesus not only died, he also lived—and he lives again.

The gospel, as the Christians called their proclamation about Jesus, addressed his death as well as his life. The four Gospels that were canonically adopted by the church give considerable attention to the death of Jesus. Though the details in their descriptions of Jesus' death differ, there is no attempt to disguise his mortality. His crucifixion by the Romans was fatal. His burial was factual. All four Gospels pronounced him dead.

Methodists, like all Christians, proclaim the message of Christ in terms of death and life. Of course, there have been times when Methodism seemed more fascinated by Jesus' death than by anything else. The ritual for Holy Communion that has been most widely used among Methodists

---

17   Ezekiel 37:10.

for centuries and that remains an authorized liturgy in The United Methodist Church today[18] puts significant emphasis on the death of Jesus. (Rooted in the Anglican liturgy that was used at the time of John Wesley, it has been seen by some critics as "a funeral for Jesus.") Methodists, for generations, have sung hymns that focused on the suffering, bleeding, dying Jesus.

In an age of popular praise music, the mortality of Jesus may be waning as a theme for singing. Yet the gospel is still a matter of death and life. To talk or sing about the Lord's death is to acknowledge our own. The prelude to resurrection life is real death. But that is a truth which most of us are neither particularly eager to experience nor inclined to understand.

When I was a young pastor of local churches, I quickly discovered a phenomenon that caught me by surprise. Palm Sunday usually drew a larger than normal congregation of worshipers. Easter, the following Sunday, had predictably the largest attendance for any Sunday of the year. But scheduling services during the intervening Holy Week on Maundy Thursday and Good Friday had to be managed with much lower expectations for attendance. Choir members might commit to sing on Maundy Thursday, but a soloist or two might be the only voices willing to sing on Good Friday. Methodists among whom I ministered would arrive in far bigger numbers for a "Triumphal Entry" on Palm Sunday and for the "Glory" of Easter than for the terrible trials of Thursday or the last words on Friday. The shadows of death are sharpened by the light of Easter sunrise, but the somber words about suffering and death, even set to music, cannot match a "Hallelujah!" Besides, it is not only Jesus' mortality that is so hard to face. It is our own.

Methodists, like all Christians, have to be honest about the gospel. It is a tale of death and life. While we have no biblical text that explicitly says Jesus laughed, we have one that says, "Jesus wept."[19] He cried at the tomb of Lazarus. He also wept over the prospects for people who fail to recognize "the things that make for peace."[20] His tears dripped with terrible pain at the death of a loved one and the destruction of a community.

What Methodists have always recognized about the gospel of Jesus

---

18 "A Service of Word and Table IV," *The United Methodist Hymnal* (Nashville: The United Methodist Publishing House, 1989), 26–31.

19 John 11:35 (KJV).

20 Luke 19:42.

Christ is its continuity that connects this life and the life to come. Salvation is a process that continues our journey before death with our journey after death. Sins are committed, confessed, and forgiven. Relationships are built, broken, and reconciled. Oppressors arise, impose their wills, and are overcome when liberation arrives with deliverance. Sometimes forgiveness and emancipation come when prophets' judgments echo in this life on earth. Sometimes they come in final judgment after death on earth. Death does not end everything, because its power does not last. The gospel continues with a message of resurrection and eternal life. Life, death, and life again are a continuous story of the process of salvation.

The continuity is the community of faith, the communion of saints. The gospel is not just for individuals. It is also for the whole people of God.

While it is not just about individuals, most Christians wonder about resurrection and eternal life in a very personal sense. Will we see and recognize the persons we have loved? What can we expect in the continuity between this life and the life to come?

The twentieth-century, neo-orthodox theologian Karl Barth said that when he got to heaven he wanted to meet all of the great theologians of other centuries—but first he wanted to meet Mozart. Barth began most days of his life listening to Mozart. He felt that the best way to enjoy life after death would also involve such sublime music in heaven.

We build our vision of life after death around the people and the perspectives that matter to us. We imagine it in terms that are familiar to us. In Jesus' time, scholars asked him about marriage in the resurrection.[21] The apostle Paul faced tough questions about a resurrection body: "How are the dead raised? With what kind of body do they come?"[22]

But first we have to face death. We have to remember that all creatures and all of their creations will die.

So the Bible is quite realistic about human mortality. We are all finite beings. One of the psalms of wisdom in the Bible says, "Our years come to an end like a sigh . . . [after] seventy years, or perhaps eighty, if we are strong."[23]

And the things that we create are finite too. With rare exceptions, such

---

21 Matthew 22:30.

22 1 Corinthians 15:35.

23 Psalm 90:9–10.

as a few pyramids in Egypt or a circle called Stonehenge in England, even the sturdiest things that humans construct will fall into ruin. And those sturdy ones may have their original purposes lost.

The same is true for the organizations that we devise to conduct our businesses, to develop our artistic imaginations, to educate our future generations, to govern our lands, and to lead our prayers. They will die.

Some of our revered religious structures were built with a sense of permanence. One can still visit Hagia Sophia, the magnificent building in Istanbul. Authorized and funded by the Byzantine Emperor Justinian nearly 1,500 years ago, it outlasted Justinian's Christian empire and the Ottoman Empire that followed. It has endured numerous earthquakes and not a few armed conflicts. It has served multiple purposes—as a church for global Christendom, then as an Eastern Orthodox cathedral, then as a Roman Catholic cathedral, then as an Orthodox cathedral again, and then as an Imperial Mosque for the Ottoman and the Turkish empires. Today, it is a museum that is formally known as Ayasofya Müzesi. The astonishing building remains. Christian mosaics and Islamic art can still be seen on its walls. But the worship that it once housed occurs there no longer. Hagia Sophia is an awesome relic, a grand ruin of great Christian and Muslim empires that live no more.

A liturgy that Methodists use to celebrate baptism and entry into the church starts with the words, "The church is of God, and will be preserved to the end of time."[24] It is an article of faith about the permanence of the Christian church as a holy community. But it does not attribute permanence to any denomination or congregation or empire—not even one that has been created in the name of Christ.

The United Methodist Church has existed only since 1968, and all Methodism has only existed in general since the early 1700s. Witnesses to the infinite are not themselves infinite. Methodism has not lived forever, nor will it likely last forever. The words of the baptism liturgy do not say that The United Methodist Church will last to the end of time.

To put this in perspective, Hagia Sophia served as a place of Christian worship for nine hundred years and then as a place for Muslim prayers for almost three hundred years before Methodism got started. Our Methodist

---

24 "The Baptismal Covenant III," *The United Methodist Hymnal*, 45.

churches, our church buildings, our churches' brand names, and our missionary institutions are finite. They can—and almost certainly will—die.

But we believe in death and life. So we believe that the church "will be preserved until the end of time." Yet we cannot be certain how long the current forms of church life will live before they die, nor can we be sure what forms of life the church will take after the present ones die. That uncertainty applies to the many manifestations of Methodism.

Of the two billion Christians in the world that are counted in thirty-four thousand different church organizations, Methodist bodies have about eighty million members. So Methodists are less than 4 percent of all Christian constituents. United Methodism is only 10 percent of the total Methodist membership. On Sunday mornings in a few sites, it may seem that Methodists are everywhere. Across the Christian world, we are not.

The peoples called Methodists are not insignificant in the mind of God. But we are a truly tiny minority among the members of the global Christian church that God will preserve to the end of time.

Does Methodism matter in the grand mission of Christianity? Will Methodism and its institutions die? What form of life will Methodism take in the age to come?

These are not abstract queries. There are fears that Methodism is dying. There should also be faith that Methodism will live. The gospel is a matter of death and life. The church's mission is a matter of death and life, conducted by bodies that will die while preaching the promise that we will live. But the currently existing forms of the faith are neither essential to, nor permanent features of, Methodism.

The history of Methodism is a tale of breakups. The arc of Methodist history is a series of straying strands, broken branches, divided paths, occasional reconciliations, and enduring divisions. If we were to sketch the story of Wesley's Methodism, it would not be a tree with many limbs but rather a stream with multiple tributaries and channels to the eternal sea, plus some lost lagoons and no small number of dry basins along the way.

In the centuries since John Wesley launched the movement, there is no straight, solid line. The popular image of Wesley as an evangelical preacher, whom crowds heard in open English fields after his heart was strangely warmed at a prayer meeting when he experienced conversion, who sent Francis Asbury to North America with instructions to "offer them Christ," and whose preachers lit the American frontier on fire for the Lord, is not an entirely false portrait. But it is hardly the whole truth.

There were forms of Methodism already present in the North American colonies before Asbury and others arrived at Wesley's invitation and direction. Thanks to lay preachers who decided to spread whatever version of Methodism they liked on their own, Wesleyan practices had begun before John Wesley sent anyone. He instructed Asbury to try to bring order to the movement. But the war for American independence interrupted the process, and the outcome of the war altered the plans.

The formal creation of a "Methodist Episcopal Church for the United States of America" happened in 1784 as an unintended result of events. The new church chose to have clergy who were ordained and to vest power in conferences of preachers.[25]

The Methodist Episcopal Church in the United States of America did not stay in its original form for very long. The first major dispute developed over race within three years after the denomination formed.[26] The first major division happened after scarcely eight years, when a preacher named James O'Kelly led a revolt against Asbury's control over the appointments of the preachers. Having lost their battle, his group seceded and formed a separate Methodist denomination. The first fracture over race[27] happened about a decade after the denomination was formed, when black Methodists led by Richard Allen left a church in Philadelphia as an act of protest against being denied the right to remain in prayer, rather than being forced to cease praying and make room for white folks. Allen and his followers formed a new Methodist denomination.

Other groups arose too. The German-speaking Evangelical Association and the United Brethren crafted their own church bodies with Wesleyan roots. But more divisions followed—over race, over power for laity, over doctrines, and over slavery. Between 1784 and 1844, there were at least six schisms that led to the creation of new denominations. The Republican Methodist Church, the African Methodist Episcopal Church, the African Methodist

---

25 Russell E. Richey, *The Methodist Conference in America* (Nashville: Kingswood, 1996), 36.

26 J. Gordon Melton, *A Will to Choose: The Origins of African American Methodism* (Lanham, MD: Rowman & Littlefield, 2007), 64.

27 Ibid., 85.

Episcopal Zion Church, the Methodist Protestant Church, and the Wesleyan Church became separate churches. In 1844, Northern and Southern Methodists severed the institutional unity of the Methodist Episcopal Church for the United States of America.

In the years that followed, other Methodist groups appeared. The Free Methodists became their own denomination in 1860. The Colored Methodist Episcopal Church[28] was formed in 1870, partly because black Methodists in the South were happy to control their own denomination and partly because whites in the Methodist Episcopal Church, South, were happy to be rid of black Methodists, many of whom were once their slaves.

More separations occurred, generating a number of religious bodies with names that have an unrecognizably Wesleyan or Methodist heritage. The Nazarene Church, the Pentecostal Holiness Churches, and the Salvation Army are a few of them.

Still others must be added to this tally. Methodist missionaries in many colonized countries brought their forms of British Methodism to a number of African nations and to Australia. Several separated sects of North American Methodism developed their mission and movements in Latin America, Asia, Africa, Eurasia, and Oceania. Some indigenous Methodisms emerged in the Caribbean and elsewhere.

Today, the World Methodist Council identifies eighty churches in 133 countries, all tracing their history to John Wesley. In the years after 1744, when Wesley first gathered a group of six preachers in a conference,[29] many institutional forms of Methodism have died. Others have come to life.

Sometimes a new Methodist form found life through the reconciliation of a few formerly separated bodies. In 1939, after decades of discussions, the Methodist Protestant Church, the Methodist Episcopal Church, and the Methodist Episcopal Church, South, achieved a reunion. Their old divisions died, and a new church came to life.

---

28 In the 1950s, the denomination changed its name to the Christian Methodist Episcopal Church in America.

29 Wesley made it clear that the word *conference* was not a description of the meeting but rather was the identity of the group that gathered. Since that first conference in 1744, Methodists (specifically their clergy) have understood a "conference" as a membership body. The basic body of The United Methodist Church, according to Division Two, Section VI, Article II of its Constitution, is the annual conference. See *The Book of Discipline of The United Methodist Church 2016*, ¶ 33, p. 35.

Yet the reunion was a façade. Behind its appealing appearance was an appalling absence of attention to the substantive divisions in Methodism.

The historically black Methodist denominations (AME, AMEZ, CME) were not part of the reunion. Moreover, the terms of the reunion included a commitment that the reunited denomination—called The Methodist Church—would be racially segregated.

In a newly devised structural pattern, the church created six "jurisdictions" for the United States. Each of them had a "jurisdictional conference," where the bishops would be elected. Five of them had regional boundaries. The sixth, designated as the "Central Jurisdiction," had racial boundaries. African-American conferences and congregations in The Methodist Church across the United States were placed in the "Central Jurisdiction." To make sure that nobody missed the point, The Methodist Church published a map of the five regional jurisdictions in the nation, then shaded and superimposed the territory of the Central Jurisdiction on the map of the country.[30]

Matters of race were not the only perplexing conflicts in finding a way toward a reunion in 1939. Gender mattered as well. During the decades after Northern and Southern Methodists were separated by the schism over slavery in 1844, women took a variety of steps in leadership of the churches. Methodist women supported the work of missionaries and expressed the view that they also were called into missionary work.

But their sense of vocation met vigorous ecclesiastical resistance. Church leaders, specifically male church leaders, blocked them. So Methodist women created their own missionary organization and sent some of their own number to the mission field. They formed the Women's Missionary Council, the Women's Foreign Missionary Society, the Women's Home Missionary Society, and the Wesleyan Service Guild.[31] The Ladies Aid Society and the Women's Society of Christian Service continued these mission ventures.

---

30 *Doctrines and Discipline of The Methodist Church 1939* (New York: The Methodist Book Concern, 1939), 448. The text in ¶ 1361, on the adjacent page 449, describes the constituent bodies of the Central Jurisdiction as follows: "The Negro Annual Conferences, the Negro Mission Conferences and Missions in the United States of America."

31 *Doctrines and Discipline of The Methodist Church 1939* (New York: The Methodist Book Concern, 1939), ¶ 1012, 1013, pp. 303ff.

Their institutional structures were financially and politically separate from the conferences that formed the units of Methodist polity.

What the women of Methodism could not control, however, were the laws of the church concerning ordinations of ministers. The Methodist Protestant Church had begun ordaining women in the late nineteenth century.[32] But that practice did not continue when The Methodist Church was formed in 1939. In effect, this reunion meant the death of full clergy rights for women. They did not come to life again until 1956.

In the saga of death and life, some things are allowed to die that should have been required to stay alive. The journey from death to life is marked with pain and suffering. Divisions can arise from many kinds of hurt. Reconciliations can inflict other harm.

In 1968, the Evangelical United Brethren—a denomination that had been formed in 1946 by the union of two bodies of German-language Wesleyans—merged with The Methodist Church to form The United Methodist Church. Coincident with their merger were efforts to end formal segregation by race in the new church.

The six jurisdictions were reduced to five. The Central Jurisdiction ended. The "Negro" churches and conferences were absorbed by the conferences and jurisdictions in their geographical regions. The new denomination created a Commission on Religion and Race to address racial and ethnic division. All this was an attempt to end segregation by causing its constitutional and legislative death, after which racial harmony would be the hallmark of the new church's life under its rewritten Constitution and *Discipline*. It did not actually succeed.

In 2018, it will have been fifty years since the officially segregated Methodist Church met its death. Yet a racially unified United Methodist Church has struggled to come to life.[33] Most United Methodist congregations gather for worship on weekends as racially homogeneous bodies. The denomination as a whole is overwhelmingly white. While significant racial diversity has come to characterize the denomination's leadership, particularly among the bishops and the general boards of the church, the same cannot be

---

32   Susan Hill Lindley, *"You Have Stept Out of Your Place": A History of Women and Religion in America* (Louisville: Westminster John Knox Press, 1996), 302, 310.

33   Joseph T. Reiff, *Born of Conviction: White Methodists and Mississippi's Closed Society* (New York: Oxford University Press, 2015).

said about local United Methodist churches. Sunday is still segregated. The Methodists' schisms that happened because of race and racism in the eighteenth and nineteenth centuries were not healed in church practice in the twentieth century or, thus far, in the twenty-first.

Meanwhile, at the moment when The United Methodist Church formed in 1968, it began building the basis for the next issue to divide the church. It found a new fissure that threatens to become a fracture.

At the time of the denomination's creation, the matter of homosexuality became a topic arousing significant debate. For fifty years, the debate has grown deeper and more divisive. Like a fault line in the church's crust, it is exerting enormous pressure. That pressure is so intense now that it could destroy this fifty-year-old denomination.

For five decades, the denomination has authorized study commissions, adopted laws, amended its Constitution, and struggled with the practices of a connectional polity that cannot impose legislative or executive uniformity. Nothing has been resolved.

In this matter of death and life, a crisis looms and questions abound. Is every human being a person of "sacred worth" as the Constitution[34] establishes and as the Social Principles of The United Methodist Church assert? Or do individuals who engage in the practice of homosexuality surrender their sacred worth by behavior that is "incompatible with Christian teaching" as the Social Principles also declare?[35] Is presiding at a service of Christian marriage for a same-sex couple so egregious that it can be a basis to expel United Methodist clergy from ordained ministry?[36] Does the inability to settle disputes over these questions mean that The United Methodist Church must die so another form of Methodism can come to life?

There are other troublesome issues. The denomination has been enduring a steady decline in membership, worship attendance, and participation in its programs of Christian education. When it was formed in 1968, The United Methodist Church claimed twelve million members who belonged to forty-two thousand local churches. Nearly fifty years later, the denomination

---

34 *The Book of Discipline of The United Methodist Church 2016*, The Constitution, Division One, Article IV, "Inclusiveness of the Church," ¶ 4, p. 26.

35 Ibid. Part V, "Social Principles," ¶ 161 G, p. 113.

36 Ibid., ¶ 2702.1(b), p. 788.

has roughly seven million members in thirty-two thousand local churches. Also, financial pressures are growing as costs of health care and retirement programs rise and as older buildings begin to fail. The average age of the members is rising. The numbers of persons who are superintending the church have declined as boundaries of the annual conferences and the districts within annual conferences expand.

The troubles are not all manifest in measurable data or statistical tables. They are also evident in the diminished footprint of The United Methodist Church in major public issues affecting society. There are virtually no big questions for which the denomination speaks with a unified voice offering vital answers. There are nearly no topics on which the denomination has a recognizable, unequivocal position. There is no sign that society looks to The United Methodist Church for solutions to problems. Answers and responses offered by the church display regional, racial, economic, political, and class differences. In some cases, on some issues, there is simply a strange silence.

Some local churches are growing. In a few cases, there are thousands—even tens of thousands—of persons gathered in congregations on Sunday. And new congregations are appearing, some of them as satellites launched by thriving local churches. Church growth is especially dramatic outside of the United States. A possibility now exists for The United Methodist Church to be a denomination with a majority of its members and a majority of its General Conference delegates coming from a continent other than North America.

Perhaps this church, focused on North American social concerns and funded by North Americans' financial resources, will die. Perhaps some other Methodism will live. These are matters of death and life. They are painful. And yet, they are strangely promising.

QUESTIONS FOR DISCUSSION

1. What events and situations in life lead people to look to the church for hope?

2. What specific things can the church offer as signs of hope?

3. Is the message of salvation for the life to come after death, or is it for this life also?

4. Is the gospel of Jesus Christ addressed only to individual persons or to social order too?

5. Is this a time of hope in the life of the church, or is this an age of doubt about its future?

6. Are conflicts in the church a threat to its mission?

7. How can the church most effectively confront the fear of death?

PART TWO

IN MEMORIAM

O Lord, we offer You
Sacrifices and prayers of praise;

Accept them on behalf of those souls
Whom we remember today.
Let them, O Lord, pass over from death to life,
As you once promised to Abraham and his seed.

Offertory from *Requiem*

OBITUARY

The Newport United Methodist Church died on Friday, June 10, 2016. Its death was expected. Born in 1885 in a northeastern Pennsylvania part of Newport Township that originally was known as Alden Station, the church was previously known as the Alden Methodist Episcopal, Alden Methodist, and Alden United Methodist Church. It was always a small congregation. Yet it had once played a significant role in its local community. Nevertheless, the Newport United Methodist Church had suffered steady declines in recent decades. Only a few active members remained. Any signs of viability had ebbed and faded some time ago. All efforts to restore vitality were futile.

The death occurred by euthanasia. In keeping with the laws and procedures of the United Methodist denomination, the Susquehanna Annual Conference of The United Methodist Church officially pronounced its death through an action to discontinue the use of the church property as a place of worship. In anticipation of discontinuance, a service of deconsecration was conducted on June 5, with persons present by invitation only. All of the church's tangible assets, including the real estate and other remains, will be released in accordance with the provisions of applicable ecclesiastical and civil law. The persons who were members of the Newport United Methodist Church at the time of its death will choose where — or whether — to transfer their memberships to another church, unless they allow the denomination's district superintendent to do so for them.

> For everything there is a season,
> and a time for every matter under heaven:
> a time to be born, and a time to die.
>
> Ecclesiastes 3:1–2

EULOGY

Some years ago, a rabbi in the Orthodox tradition of American Judaism said that it was a common practice at funerals in his community for a few grains of soil from the land of Israel to be placed in the coffin of the deceased. For the Jews of the Diaspora, this rabbi said, it matters not where they have lived and studied and worked and raised their families. The land of Israel, he said, is still their home.

Other migrating peoples relate to their ethnic, religious, and ancestral places of origin much more loosely. Home becomes wherever they have moved, wherever they have settled, and wherever the next generations—not the prior ones—study, work, and play. They reside, they start schools, and they develop burial grounds for their dead.[1] Their culture—including the cuisine and the common tongue of the old country—might be cultivated for a few generations. But it happens on new soil in a new home.

Alden Station was a railroad stop in the southern part of Luzerne County in the late nineteenth and early twentieth centuries. Like much of northeastern Pennsylvania, it offered a place where migrants from coal mining regions of Europe could find familiar terrain and toil. Coal companies acquired the land but needed labor to extract from the earth the shiny, sulfurous carbon. Rail companies acquired rights-of-way and other land, on which they moved the coal. The migrant miners and their families were lured by the prospects of steady work, company-owned housing they could rent, company-owned stores where they could shop, and company-owned land on which they could build their houses of worship according to the religious traditions that they brought with them.

Alden Station was one of those places. In public settings—at work, at the store, in school—the migrants sought ways to meld into a community. In church, they saw ways to celebrate in their separate traditions.

From the houses that sat on the hillside, on Monday through Friday, the children could walk to the elementary school. On Sunday, their extended families could walk to the Russian Orthodox Church, the Episcopal Church, or the Methodist Church. Roman Catholics had to go only slightly farther. Their church buildings occupied land that was either donated by or acquired from a coal operator or a rail line.

In Alden Station, the church building on the highest point of the hill belonged to the Methodists. Its initial members were English, Cornish, and Welsh immigrants. For two or three generations, their children and grandchildren followed them up that hill and into the life of their church.

Being Methodist was not merely a cultural or familial habit. It was their choice for missional purposes. The Methodist movement, founded in

---

1   One way to show that an immigrant group has decided to shift its primary identity from the old country to the new one is the evidence that they have established a cemetery. That act is a sign of determining, "This is where we will live, and this is where we will die."

England by John Wesley, had given considerable attention to miners and their working-class families in England, Cornwall, and Wales. Low-level laborers not only felt welcomed in Methodist societies but also discovered that Methodist preachers went to the pits and places where they labored. Where a mine opened, a Methodist preacher arrived. Where a gas explosion or rock fall caused casualties, Methodist preachers offered pastoral care and comfort. The evangelical agenda of the Methodists was to meet the spiritual as well as the physical and social needs of the workers and their families.

Methodism supported education and health care for the coal miners' households. Methodism democratized doctrine and made it accessible through music so the illiterate who could not read about the means of grace could sing about them. Methodism offered even the poor, who could not afford "church dues" or "pew rent," a home in a system of discipline for practicing the faith. Methodism connected small communities with a larger regional, national, and global mission through people whom they would never see. In the Methodist form of apostolic ministry,[2] preachers were appointed by a connectional system and traveled to places of service. A Methodist minister, called a "traveling preacher,"[3] was sent to a community, called a "charge," and not just to a congregation.

This may have had massive significance in the land where John Wesley founded the movement. It has been argued that one reason the French Revolution did not cross the channel and become an English revolution was that the English social classes likely to rise against privileged classes felt empowered by Methodism to shape their political destinies.[4]

When nineteenth-century immigrants from England, Cornwall, and

---

2   Richey, "United Methodist Doctrine," pp. 35–38.

3   Richard P. Heitzenrater, *Wesley and the People Called Methodists* (Nashville: Abingdon, 1995), 184. The phrase was established in the Constitution of The Methodist Church when it was formed in 1939, and was used as the title of a chapter in the first set of laws adopted by that reunited church. (See *Doctrines and Discipline of The Methodist Church 1939* [New York: The Methodist Publishing House, 1939], ¶¶ 21, 211–41). The phrase still appears in the Constitution of The United Methodist Church and in current church law (see *The Book of Discipline of The United Methodist Church 2016*, ¶¶ 27.6, 31.7, 604.6, pp. 33, 34, 413–14).

4   Elissa S. Itzkin, "The Halévy Thesis—A Working Hypothesis? English Revivalism: Antidote for Revolution and Radicalism, 1789–1815" (*Church History*, vol. 44, no. 1, pp. 47–56, 1975). J. W. Walsh, "Elie Halévy and the Birth of Methodism," *Transactions of the Royal Historical Society* (1975), Fifth Series, vol. 25, pp. 1–20.

Wales made their way to Alden Station, they found an American version of Methodism that affirmed their dreams and supported their interests: labor unions for the workers; public schools for their children; a missionary spirit that led to the creation of community hospitals for the sick, the injured, or the dying; and institutions for the care of orphans.

So the families that climbed the hill in Alden Station to their Methodist building were on a mission. They were going to hear and study the Word of the Lord. They were going to receive the sacraments, sing praises, and seek salvation. They were connected to each other, to their local community, and to a global mission in a social system. And they were finding meaning, dignity, discipline, and purpose in their lives on earth.

My mother walked that hill with her big sister. It was where their father had been raised and where he had, as a boy, mastered the art of carrying growlers from the miners' saloon up the hill to his alcoholic father. It was where my mother and her sister learned, from their earliest days, to grieve for the older brother whom they never knew. He had died in infancy during the influenza epidemic on February 14, 1919—Valentine's Day. There was no cemetery near the church on top of the hill. So his body lies in a grave on another hillside, near a different Methodist church, where his mother (my grandmother) had been raised and where she put his remains beneath a stone marker with a lamb carved on top. For the remaining sixty years of her life, my grandmother hated Valentine's Day. When I was born, a generation after his death, I was given her son's first and middle names.

An inconsolable grief burdened my grandparents' hearts and minds, but they bore it every Sunday when they climbed the hill with their daughters in Alden Station to the Methodist church. They went for worship and sat in Sunday school. My mother and her sister joined the activities of the Epworth League. My grandmother was in the Women's Society of Christian Service, or WSCS. My grandfather was in the Men's Bible Class.

At the same time, my father and his four siblings walked that same hill. But his family did more than attend and join the Alden Methodist Episcopal Church—as it was known until the reunion of three Methodist denominations in 1939 changed its name to Alden Methodist Church. My father's parents were the custodians of the building. It was a responsibility that involved the whole family. They cleaned, dusted, mopped, and swept the church interior every week. They mowed the lawn in summer and shoveled the snow in winter. And, on cold Sunday mornings, they climbed the hill very early to get the coal fire started so the building would be warm for worship.

Nobody was excluded from the obligations, and there were no excused absences from the work. My father, who was the middle child of five, learned that lesson the hard way. He told me that he got really drunk only one time in his life. It was in the spring of 1937, just after his nineteenth birthday. The Newport High School boys' basketball team won the state championship on a Saturday night in the capital city, Harrisburg.

My father, who had dropped out of school in the eighth grade, was part of a group that took the train to see the game. Apparently there was plenty of beer on the ride home, and my father consumed more than his share of it. Around four on Sunday morning, he rolled into bed.

About an hour later, he felt a cold rag on his face and heard his father's voice say that what he did on Saturday night was his own business but what he was going to do on Sunday morning was family business. Barely awake and scarcely sober, he had to climb the hill and care for his chores at the church.

So my mother and father were raised in the same church. It was where they went to Sunday school and where they sat with their families in worship. It was from the perspective of the church on the hill that they saw the nation and their neighbors cope with the Depression in the 1930s. They saw unemployed men, hired by the Works Progress Administration, lay bricks on the streets of the hill to smooth the dirt and gravel roadways. They also saw WPA workers build a retaining wall of stone around their church as a way not only to improve the community and the church property but also to give each unemployed person who worked on it the dignity of a job.

And it was from the perspective of the church on the hill that they played active roles in the wider world, when it was engulfed in war. They and their friends—most of the boys and also a few of the girls—got military uniforms when the World War II draft became nearly universal. My father was one of the draftees.

My mother and father never held membership in any other church. It was the site of their wedding in 1944, just before my father's Army unit was deployed to the Pacific Theater for eighteen months. It was the site where their children—my sister and I—were baptized and were raised to be believers. And it was also the site of our parents' funerals: our father's in 1992 and our mother's in 2010.

The church on top of the hill in Alden nurtured generations of us through hunger, the Depression, and war. It housed our youth meetings, our scout groups, and more dinners for fund-raising and fellowship than anyone could ever count. It shaped us for life. And it connected us to the larger, global Christian enterprise that spanned two millennia.

Among the earliest leaders of Christianity was a North African named Cyprian,[5] who lived in the third century. In his treatise on the unity of the church, Cyprian wrote, "He can no longer have God for his Father who has not the Church for his mother."

In the year 258, Cyprian was condemned, exiled, and executed for running afoul of the imperial authorities. They found aspects of his writing and teaching objectionable. Nonetheless, his words endured. In 1536, the Reformation leader John Calvin quoted Cyprian in his *Institutes of the Christian Religion*. In 1843, a Pennsylvania farmer and theologian named John Williamson Nevin quoted Cyprian in a book titled *The Anxious Bench*, which was his argument against the revivalist techniques that were the religious fad of the day.

Today, Cyprian's metaphor for the church is troublesome for its sexism. But Cyprian had a point. The church provides scriptures, creeds, liturgies, prayers, and systems of discipline to guide people through life. The church cares for people in the name of God's justice, mercy, and peace. The church patiently nurtures with parental love anyone who seeks to become a disciple of Jesus Christ in the world.

It was the people called Methodists in that church on the hill who nurtured me, who indeed mothered me, from the day I was baptized until the day I was set free to continue my spiritual journey elsewhere. And most of the nurturing was done by women, whose complex lives cannot be reduced to stereotypes and whose profound commitment of spiritual energy deserves to be honored.

In fact, Newport United Methodist Church—by its final name and by all the other names that came before—needs to be eulogized for the ways it mothered so many. Much of the mothering was done by women, whose only recognition is to be remembered.

---

5   The writings of Cyprian were on the authorized list of books that Wesley wanted the superintendents of the Methodist preachers to read, according to "The Minutes" of his first conference in 1744. *The Works of John Wesley: The Methodist Societies, The Minutes of Conference*, vol. 10, ed. Rack, 144.

There was Gertrude Fairchild, who handled the nursery class every Sunday and who helped the Methodist Youth Fellowship lead an Easter Sunrise Service every spring. During the rest of her time, on mornings after her husband Harry went to work around the coal mines, she managed her family's general store, struggling to keep it in business.

There was Esther Roman, who taught the first and second grade class on Sunday and taught in the public schools on other days. It was from her that generations of young children learned the benediction that God told Moses to use in blessing his brother Aaron:

> The Lord bless you and keep you;
> the Lord make his face to shine upon you, and be gracious to you;
> the Lord lift up his countenance upon you, and give you peace.[6]

To those words from the book of Numbers, Mrs. Roman immediately added, "See everybody next Sunday." I learned the benediction of Aaron with the Roman addendum.

There was Dorothy Richards, who taught the older elementary class on Sundays, served as the lead soprano in the church choir, and tutored students during other days. There was Ruth Moyer, who worked tirelessly with the youth fellowship, encouraging our efforts to raise funds in a Harvest Festival for the Methodist Children's Home, which had been established to care for orphaned children in our annual conference area. There was Edna Cherrie, who led the Women's Society of Christian Service (WSCS), helping the adults and the children of the church to feel some connection to the global missionary enterprise in Methodism. There was Mabel Turner, who led assemblies for everyone in the Sunday school so the children could learn the beliefs of the church the same way the adults did—by singing it. There were Alta Becker, who played the organ, and her sister Reba Davis, who led the children's choir.

There was some combination of women who rehearsed with the children for several weeks prior to Christmas Eve, when an annual pageant or play featuring every available child drew parents and grandparents into the sanctuary. They were also the women who, in the weeks before Christmas, made sure that we filled cardboard stockings with dimes for the

---

6   Numbers 6:24–26.

Methodist Hospital in Brooklyn, New York, where Methodists would provide care for patients in a big, distant city. Collectively, the church mothered us in the faith through such women.

The men participated in other ways. Some were our teachers. Some used their physical labor and technical training to maintain the plumbing, heating, and electrical systems. Some had other specialized skills.

There was Art Moyer, who had been a cook in the army during World War II and who knew how to organize a church supper when a few hundred people were going to be served turkey, mashed potatoes, and vegetables. And there were a few men who tried to be entertainers.

At least one of their efforts was a sign of just how strong the power of sin can be. In the 1930s, some of the young men of Alden Methodist Episcopal Church did a minstrel show. Though I never witnessed their performance, I have seen photographic evidence. Apparently, it was popular enough that people felt proud to keep a picture of the cast for decades on the wall that every worshiper would pass when approaching the sanctuary on Sunday morning. I saw the photo every week. There was my father, with his fellow cast members, in black face on the stage of the same room where the church had dinners and gathered for Sunday school.

As a child, I found the photo odd. As an adult, I found it painfully embarrassing, hurtful, and sinful. So I asked my sister if she, as an active member of the church, could find a way to have the photo removed. As an academic historian, I know that photo must be preserved in the archives as evidence of the sin of racism that is so insidious even a little Methodist church in the North could find it entertaining.

Those same young men, who wore black face and who sat on the stage of Alden's Sunday school room for a photograph of the cast in the minstrel show, stood outside the church one Sunday in 1937 for another photo with multiple generations of men who were their fathers and grandfathers and siblings and friends. It was taken in the same year that Newport won the state basketball championship.

According to the caption on that photograph, they were the Men's Bible Class of the Alden Methodist Episcopal Church. They stood on the steps of the church, flanked by the stone wall that the WPA had built. It may have been the largest group of men ever to be considered members of the Men's Bible Class. Every time I look at the sixty-six men in that photo, I can see my father (who would have been nineteen years old), his older brother, both of my grandfathers, the brothers and brothers-in-law of my grandfathers, a co-owner of the plumbing company where my father worked for nearly all of his career, a number of my public school teachers, a few men who were old enough to have personal memories of their fathers' tales about the Civil War, and a lot of young men who would be receiving—less than five years later—their draft notices for service in World War II.

On a wall of the same room where we had Sunday school, where we ate countless church dinners, where I attended Scout meetings, and where the cast of the minstrel show sat for a photo, there was a plaque bearing the names of "our boys" who served in World War II. The names of my father and his two brothers were on the plaque.

So was the name Keith Jeffries, notable for the star next to his name. He had been aboard the USS Arizona when it sank in Pearl Harbor on December 7, 1941. Entombed in the ship, his body was never brought back to Alden for a funeral.

About twenty years later, I was in the high school class, which was taught by James Jeffries, the father of the late Keith Jeffries. An older man who yearned to teach the Bible to boys, he had long since lost the ability to control a class. His dementia—which we could recognize but for which we did not yet have a name—precluded him from understanding our adolescent efforts to ignore him. I regret, to this day, that we did not show him the honor or respect he deserved.

At the time all of this was being lived, it was hard to comprehend. But it is clearer now. The church on the hill, which became known in its last years as the Newport United Methodist Church, expended its resources in introducing generations of people to faith, discipleship, worship, fellowship, order, chaos, class, life, dementia, death, and an array of so many other aspects of ordinary human life. This church was our extended family.

When my sister and I entered the sanctuary on a typical Sunday for worship with our parents, we took one of the pews to the left of the center aisle. Around us on all sides were our neighbors and our relatives. Nearest us were my mother's parents, my mother's sister, her husband, and their daughter. On the other side of the aisle were my father's parents. Near them were two of my father's siblings: his unmarried sister and his older brother, who sat with his wife and their three children.

Ours was not the only multigenerational family who lived on the hillside below the church, or on the streets nearby, and who gathered there for worship. There was a girl named Debbie, who had been diagnosed with diabetes when she was a very small child. We learned from her and her parents, who managed an appliance store in Alden, that children sometimes are stricken by major illnesses, which can be debilitating or deadly.

There was a young man named Bill, whose parents recognized that he had some amazing gifts. He played a marimba, a percussion instrument similar to a xylophone. For a while during his college years, he directed the church choir. And we had a chance to learn something from him when he traveled a path that none of us ever previously dreamed we could take. We learned from him that one could have an intellectual and personal horizon far beyond the hillside of Alden Station and that one could bring a reasoning mind to our spiritual beliefs. After completing college, Bill did something that nobody in that congregation had ever done or had ever imagined doing. He earned a PhD. He went to work for the National Institutes of Health, and he served for a time as one of its directors.

We learned a lot about life in that church as children, including a few things we might have preferred (or our parents might have preferred) that we not know. We learned that families function with a lot of internal tension. We learned that siblings struggle with each other at every age and stage of life — fighting with one another as children, feuding in adulthood. Childhood disputes might involve ownership of toys or affection from the parents. Adult siblings' disputes might involve rights over inheritances of private property or political power.

And yet, in a small church in a small town, the opponents might be — in fact they often were — seated in the same sanctuary on Sundays. They sang from the same hymnal and took the Sacrament from the same chancel rail, before heading in separate directions after the benediction was spoken and the bell resounded from its perch in the tower.

We learned that social rank and class matter. And we also learned that, while such things can divide churches and communities, the divisions can be transcended.

Most Sundays, on the side of the sanctuary across the aisle from where my sister and I sat, were a woman and man who co-owned the plumbing company that employed my father. Their name was Turner. It was the same as my mother's maiden name. One of my father's often-repeated jokes was that he only learned she was not a member of the rich Turner family after they were married. Tom and Fannie Turner drove a Cadillac to church on

Sundays. In the winter, on some Sunday mornings when it was cold, she wore a mink coat to worship. In summer, he wore a tan suit and white shoes to worship.

As a child, I marveled at what it would mean for a man to own more than one pair of dress shoes or for a woman to wear a winter coat that was not only for warmth but also for style. On cold Sundays, my mother wore the one winter coat that she owned, and its purpose was to keep her warm. A wealthier woman, I realized, could wear a coat that showed class in addition to keeping warm.

Yet I also knew that the Turners (the rich ones with the Cadillac) were unfailingly kind to me. And I later learned that they were unfailingly generous to the church. Though they could have driven their Cadillac to other, bigger churches where they would worship with people in their own socioeconomic class, they never did. The congregation and the community and the Methodist connection meant more to them than their social rank.

Moreover, on Sunday mornings, distinctions of class tended to disappear. Maybe the rich Turners owned many more than one set of dress clothes. But a person could only wear one coat or one pair of shoes at a time. We dressed not to be compared with others but to be at our finest in whatever set of church clothes we had available.

So, every Sunday, it was part of my father's routine to make sure that his dress shoes had a bright shine. And every Monday, when he was back in the work clothes that were typical for any plumber, my mother laundered and starched his white shirt so it would be stiffly ready for the next weekend. When the collar frayed, she unstitched and "turned" it. Then she starched and ironed it again.

During the workweek, people like my father wore clothes that were soiled and smelly and sweaty because of the jobs they had to do. My mother wore either the crisp white uniform of a nurse, when she was working in a hospital, or the casual cotton that was simply comfortable for tending to things at home. But on Sunday morning, there was only one social class. And everybody in it was determined to look her or his best.

So the church on the top of the hill in Alden Station formed us in the faith. It also created a sense of unity that transcended social class. And it opened windows to a world beyond the boundaries of our own community. My maternal grandfather was one who gazed through those windows quite often. He was uneducated in any formal sense. He held neither a degree nor a diploma. But he was tutored in a technical sense, with an exceptional understanding of electricity and of electrical motors. He moved from being a miner to being, eventually, the chief electrician for the coal company that employed him. The motors that ran pumps to keep water from flooding the mine tunnels and the motors that ran air handlers to keep explosive gas from filling the underground chambers were his responsibility. If a pump or an air handler quit during the night, he was called to work.

He loved technical manuals with texts and diagrams about electrical machinery. They were the sacred scriptures for his trade, and he poured endlessly over them. But he also loved to read more widely in fiction and nonfiction, including books on baseball. As a young man, he was a semipro pitcher. He never lost his affection for the game.

He also enjoyed hearing sermons from famous preachers. After worship at Alden every Sunday, he went home and tuned the radio to hear a sermon from Harry Emerson Fosdick at Riverside Church in New York or some other preacher after Fosdick retired.

I doubt that he agreed with Fosdick on many theological matters. But agreement was irrelevant for a man with deep hunger for the things of the Spirit, which he wanted to savor even if the food being offered was not his favorite. He wanted to learn from others.

Yet there was one topic on which he tolerated no dissent. My grandfather was a Methodist because of his commitment to the mission of temperance, he insisted. He lived with the memory that, as a child, he had been the one who carried alcohol up the hill for his father to consume at home. That memory scarred him. He was a Methodist because he embraced a personal and social discipline. He said, "Methodists stand for Prohibition."

In that, he had something in common with a Methodist whom he never could have met and with whom he probably would have disagreed on many things. Frances Willard, a perennial activist and prototypical feminist, held a number of views with which my grandfather may have differed. But they were Methodists who shared the denomination's commitment to temperance. It was the movement that built the Methodist building, which is on Capitol Hill, and to which my grandfather probably contributed. Temperance was a movement in which Methodism joined forces with other evangelical churches to pass the Prohibition Amendment. And when Prohibition ended, temperance was a movement that Methodism was still determined to keep within its mission.

Constitutional Prohibition ended in the United States in 1933. But, for the mission of connectional Methodism that meant so much to people like Frances Willard, the cause of temperance was vital. To my grandfather, the power of prohibition endured. That the US Constitution had been changed was inconsequential from his perspective. He had learned as a boy that small amounts of "the drink" could deprive a child of shoes or a family of a meal. Mention of a social drink appalled him. "Nobody ever became an alcoholic without being a social drinker first," he repeatedly said.

It was Methodism that, in my grandfather's view, had broken the alcoholic cycle that had harmed his childhood. It was Methodism's mission to keep alcohol from hurting other families and from harming the social order. So he was a Methodist by choice. He wanted his children and their children to be committed to this larger Methodist mission as well—not just for the sake of his extended household, but for the sake of all human life. The Methodist connection put him in touch with the wider nation and the whole world.

Whether he was right or wrong in his attitude to alcohol is beside the point. He looked at the world beyond his own work, beyond his own neighborhood, beyond his own family, and beyond his own educational limitations. What he saw was that Methodism's mission could have some positive impact on things far beyond his own personal life.

Other members of the church in Alden Station also used Methodism as a means to glimpse a larger horizon. Some ministers did as well. In the structures of the church during my childhood, only ordained ministers had the authority to administer the sacraments. Any preacher who was not yet fully ordained might be appointed to serve at Alden. But Baptism and Holy Communion required someone with full credentials—a retired minister, the district superintendent, or some other ordained elder—to preside at the sacraments. On such Sundays, often once a quarter, we felt connected to Methodism's bigger system, and we felt that it was connected to us.

One Sunday afternoon, when I was still in elementary school, our parents decided to take the family to Central Methodist Church in Wilkes-Barre, about twelve miles from home. It was the biggest church building in the biggest city we had nearby. It was one of those very rare Sundays when my sister, our parents, and I stayed in our Sunday best suits and dresses for the whole day.

We were going to attend the annual conference, where the bishop would preach and the ministers would learn what their appointments would be for the coming year. We sat in a pew just in front of one of the ministers, who was a cousin of my father and who had also been raised by the church on the hill in Alden.

At the conclusion of his sermon, Bishop Fred Pierce Corson invited young people to come forward and agree to join him along with the rest of the Methodist connection in Christian mission. He asked us to accept an opportunity to become "Bishop's Crusaders." Among others, I went forward. The bishop put a small, silver, Celtic cross in my hand. And I became, in yet another way, a participant in the larger Methodist mission.

Then we heard the bishop read the appointments. We listened to learn where my father's cousin would be moving and who our preacher would be for the coming year. We went home, knowing that the Methodist connection included us in Alden.

All of our ministers at Alden in my youth rode a circuit of three churches every Sunday morning. Some were still finishing their theological education, so they were also commuting to school during the week. To a certain extent that was a burden for the local church, since board or committee meetings had to be on Friday nights or when the pastor was in town. But it also meant that the minister had access to persons and issues beyond the hillside surrounding the church building. Sermons became much more interesting if a preacher referred to things of spiritual significance for the world beyond Alden.

One of those theological students who was appointed as our minister was Douglas Neal Akers. He brought youthful enthusiasm and emotional energy to his ministry. Doug and his wife also brought, for the first time in many members' memories, a young family. They moved into the parsonage that was located next to one of the other local churches on the three-point charge.

Marilyn and Doug had married before he completed his undergraduate degree. For most of his time as our pastor, he attended seminary, driving with two or three others on Mondays from northeastern Pennsylvania to Washington, DC, and then back on Fridays after a week of studies at Wesley Theological Seminary. Marilyn and he had a daughter, Susan, who we soon learned had been born with cystic fibrosis. Caring about her and coping with her condition became part of the church's life. We experienced the church as an extended family even further when they had a second daughter, to whom they gave a middle name "Ruth," for an Alden church leader by that name, Doug said. The Akers's presence modeled a family that could give as well as receive care. But his impact as a minister went beyond the personal.

Doug's sermons, on more than a few memorable occasions, had a prophetic edge that challenged the little congregation to think deeply about big issues. One such sermon, which he delivered around the time of the 1960 presidential election, acknowledged the puzzling problem for many Protestants in Pennsylvania, who were facing a prospect that a Roman Catholic might be chosen for the White House. He addressed the issue through a text that opens the thirteenth chapter of Paul's letter to the Romans, "Let everyone be subject to the governing authorities, for ... those authorities that exist have been instituted by God." The young preacher pressed the little church to ponder whether such a word in Scripture means that the process of an election in a democracy is an invitation to discern and to take part in God's will.

On another occasion, he took issue with one of the revered hymns of the church. Noting that "Are Ye Able?" was beloved by both older adults and members of the youth fellowship, he called attention to the question, "Are ye able ... to be crucified with Me?" Then he called attention to the hymn's answer, "Lord, we are able!" And he prodded us to acknowledge the hymn's hypocrisy, since few if any of us were willing or ready or able to be victims of capital punishment if defending our Christian faith might require it. "I can't sing that hymn anymore with you," he said.

On still another occasion, he did something in the pulpit that had never happened before, to anyone's knowledge. He arranged to bring one of his seminary classmates back to Alden as a guest preacher. That young visitor in the pulpit made a big impression, not all of it necessarily positive, with his sermon on what it means to be a Christian disciple as seen through the lives of the Twelve whom Jesus had called to follow him during his earthly life. It was not so much the content of the sermon that cast an impression on the congregation that day. It was the color of the guest preacher's skin. Nobody could recall any previous occasion on which a black person brought the word of the Lord (or, for that matter, had been in attendance to hear the word of the Lord) in that place.

In the few years that Doug Akers served as the pastor of the Alden church on the charge, he made direct impacts on individual members and on the institution. When he completed his seminary education, he was appointed elsewhere, and he became a full-time pastor instead of a part-time student-pastor. But the people of Alden and the Akers family never really felt disconnected. He had led the local church in a project to renovate the sanctuary, shifting from a central pulpit and a subordinated Communion table to a split chancel with the table at the center. He confronted people in the annual conference who, in his judgment, had misplaced their priorities in a fund-raising project to support a home for orphaned or neglected children: they focused on the *fun* in raising funds, he said, instead of on the mission to care for children. He chastised all the clergy who controlled annual conference affairs for being shortsighted in their assessments of young candidates for the ordained ministry.

To the end of its days as an active church, Alden (or Newport) still had sanctuary features that Doug Akers led the congregation to affirm with their votes as well as their funds. The people of Alden continued to feel close to Susan Akers to the end of her days, until she succumbed to cystic fibrosis as a girl in her early teens. And, years later, to a degree that strains the capacity for empathy, the people on the hill prayerfully shared the pain that Doug and Marilyn endured, when their second daughter (the one whose middle name was "Ruth" and who by then was a public school teacher in Syracuse, New York) was murdered by an intruder who assaulted her in her apartment as she arrived at home after attending the funeral of her grandfather—Doug's father.

Doug had ministered to the Alden church. The church had ministered to him and his family. Together, he and the church had walked through the valley of the shadow of death. Then they both died. A few weeks before the annual conference met and declared the Newport United Methodist Church dead, Doug died of cancer. The same session of the annual conference that discontinued the little church on the hill in Alden also offered prayers that Doug would find eternal rest among the saints, who already included his two daughters and countless parishioners.

Before, during, and after Doug served as its pastor, the little church in Alden had nurtured many generations of members to cope with many matters of death and life. Coal miners died at work. A young man died in war. Children died of disease. Nevertheless, the saints persisted, believing that death does not have the final word.

NECROPSY

People are not immune to death. We know that age and illness can claim a life, and we have practiced how to cope when a person dies of a disease. But what causes a church to descend to such depths that it has to be put to death, and how do we cope with that? Can institutions that foster sacred space in the world reach the point that they have to die? Living organisms are programmed by their biology to cease living. But is it also true for living organizations? Christianity is built on a foundation of faith in eternal life. But is it necessary for communities formed by faithful Christians to fall into ruin before they rise in resurrection? How do Christian communities die? How did the one in Alden deteriorate to the point that it had to be euthanized?

The answers clearly cannot be found in the political rhetoric of the age to which so many of us so easily turn. Neither a "liberal" nor a "conservative" explanation is of any use. The church in Alden did not dissolve into a cesspool of secularism in the sixties, as conservatives are wont to say is what slays mainstream churches. It did not abandon needs of the poor or the rights of labor or public education, as liberals are wont to assert is what cost their congregations' credibility. It did not ignore the interests of the young or desert the interests of the old. Its members pressed for abstinence from alcohol, and they also pressed for participation in organized labor. They did liberal things and conservative things, supported scout groups, sent draftees to war, welcomed veterans back home, gave comfort to the grieving, and sought ways through the walls of religious bigotry that had been built between Protestants and Catholics. Ten years after the end of World War II, in which so many of their sons had fought the Japanese, members welcomed home a young man who served in Korea and who came back with a bride he had met in Tokyo. This was a church with a living faith. When its death came, the cause was not that its living faith had died. Something else had happened.

Methodism has been built with a somewhat complex structure. It can be traced, at least in part, to a connectional system of church polity, which was devised by its founder, John Wesley. Basically, he deployed his preachers to regions with responsibility for the Methodist ministry in that locality. It was a workable and understandable scheme, and it coexisted nicely with the parish system of the established Church of England, in which Mr. Wesley was ordained to the priesthood. Parishes were geographical territories. So were the Methodist "charges" to which the preachers were sent. Before appointment, they faced examinations by their peers and superiors, who judged them to have met the criteria for membership in the conference that Wesley had conceived.

It functioned suitably in the early days of American Methodism, with preachers sent to their appointments where they were held accountable for the fruits of their labors within the bounds of their pastoral charges. As the American frontier moved, so did the itinerant preachers, who were sent to travel their appointed circuits. Mechanisms were put in place to educate and prepare them for these ministries.

But there were complications in this system. One was racism that, in concert with slavery, led Methodists to decide whether black and white constituents had to be treated separately—if not differently. Another was mobility, with frequent relocations or moves that could be managed by young, single preachers but not by those with families. Another was success, as Methodism was growing in numbers across the socioeconomic strata of American life. Historian Kenneth Rowe often remarked that one of the biggest challenges affecting Methodism occurred as it moved "from the back streets to Main Street."

By the middle of the nineteenth century, Methodists' distinctive "societies" and "camp meetings" and "class meetings" had begun shifting into "congregational" life. By the middle of the twentieth century, the "local church"[7] had become nearly normative.

Most Methodist churches were in rural areas, villages, and small towns, where Methodism reflected the life and economy of the region. Methodism had vitality when connected to the communities that did not have a means to be vigorous on their own. The Methodists in Alden Station formed such a community church.

What created their community was coal—a harder, rarer, lower sulfur version of the carbon that has long been mined in most of the continents on the planet. Known as "anthracite" or "hard coal" or "rock coal," it was distinctively and abundantly found in northeastern Pennsylvania. It had a rare quality. It could be used indoors to heat homes.

Most coal could only be burned in open forges like those in blacksmiths'

---

7   The phrase "local church" was a twentieth-century invention for America's Methodists. The term does not exist in the *Doctrines and Discipline of the Methodist Episcopal Church 1924* or *The Discipline of The Methodist Episcopal Church, South 1922*. When Northern and Southern Methodists were reunited with the Methodist Protestant Church, *Doctrines and Discipline of The Methodist Church 1939* had a full chapter on "The Local Church."

shops or in big airy furnaces, like those at industrial centers or aboard moving steam engines such as ships at sea and trains on rails. In smaller enclosed spaces, such as private residences, the typical products of combustion from most coal fires (sulfurous gases and smoke, for example) produced unpleasant or hazardous environmental consequences.

But in 1808, an innkeeper named Jesse Fell was able to burn anthracite on a grate inside his tavern in Wilkes-Barre, Pennsylvania. A small grate could burn anthracite in a fireplace and heat a room. A bigger grate in a furnace with forced air could heat a house. Fell's discovery, about twelve miles from the hill where the Methodists would build the Alden church nearly eighty years later, changed the region.

In the decades following Jesse Fell's success, the anthracite coal industry began to flourish. Residences could have central heating systems rather than relying on individual room fireplaces. Kitchens stoves could maintain reasonably consistent temperatures for cooking, roasting, and baking indoors. Job opportunities for laborers in the mines and on the ground expanded. Land values rose because of the anthracite lying below the surface. Immigrants from coal mining countries arrived to seek work. And soon their churches grew.

The latter half of the nineteenth century and the first quarter of the twentieth century brought waves of immigrants: Methodists (from England, Cornwall, and Wales), Catholics (from Poland, Lithuania, Slovakia, Italy, Ireland, and elsewhere), and Orthodox Christians (from Ukraine, Russia, and elsewhere). They came to northeastern Pennsylvania. For about a hundred years, coal was king in that part of the country.[8]

The small coal mining towns discovered the need—and the capacity—to support multiple churches. Some were differentiated not just by their ecclesial traditions but also by their ethnicity. In the little coal town of Glen Lyon,[9] where I went to junior high, Methodists had a small church building. It

---

8   The front page of each daily newspaper published the mine schedule for the ensuing day. A mine operator would release word, stating whether the operations for the next day would be "working" or "idle" or were still "undecided." Such information was printed daily until the middle of the 1960s. Newscasters on radio updated the information for the benefit of miners and their families.

9   Glen Lyon was the setting for *The Miracle of the Bells*, a film starring Fred MacMurray, Alida Valli, Frank Sinatra, and Lee J. Cobb. Scenes were filmed in Glen Lyon and at area churches. Released in 1948, its producers hired a number of Glen Alden company coal miners as extras. One of them was my paternal grandfather, who received a $5.00 check from RKO for his work. He never cashed his "souvenir" check.

was dwarfed by three large Roman Catholic structures, each of which was the parish home for a different ethnic constituency.

In the adjacent small city of Nanticoke, church buildings were landmarks. The Presbyterians and Episcopalians each had one. Baptists developed several congregations. Roman Catholics had numerous parishes, each with a distinct ethnic identity and a few of which operated parochial schools. Two Methodist churches built structures, one linked to the mainstream denomination and another connected to the Primitive Methodist Church, a sect that arose from a nineteenth-century theological dispute.

Coal was king. Other industries offered employment opportunities too. Fabrics were formed into garments in small sewing factories that occupied workspaces on floors above retail shops. Mills made specialized materials such as silk thread. Machine shops produced steel cables and industrial equipment. Railroads moved coal. And northeastern Pennsylvania had factories that rolled cigars and two major breweries.

The people who did the work typically were organized into unions. That brought bigger incomes, better working conditions, broader assessments of skills required for the jobs, and greater dignity for their labors. In the needle trades, skilled workers belonged to the International Ladies Garment Workers Union (ILGWU). In the construction specialties, plumbers and carpenters and painters belonged to craft unions affiliated with the American Federation of Labor (AFL). Teamsters focused on getting truck drivers and warehouse workers into organized labor. Most significant for the area was the United Mine Workers, who did more to improve the wages and working conditions of miners than any other force in society, according to my grandfather.

Beyond these industries, service operations of various kinds thrived. Nanticoke had a bustling retail business on its main streets. Public transportation offered a means to reach the shops and stores. Professional schools and colleges opened under the auspices of religious orders and other private organizations. Theaters, movie houses, and arenas offered boxing, vaudeville, circuses, and other entertainments. Hospitals provided health care, particularly for miners and their families. Medical professionals found jobs. And almost all of these people found the need for religious institutions. Churches thrived.

When the Depression arrived in the 1930s, it severely affected all of these elements in the society. The terrible economic situation left very few unscathed. Ironically, the decade of the 1930s was really the apex of population and community life in the region.

No one could have known it at the time, but the region had reached its peak in the years when World War II was erupting in Europe. Soon that conflict and another in the Pacific enfolded every American, including the Methodists in Alden, their neighbors in Nanticoke, and the rest of Luzerne County in northeastern Pennsylvania. The war effort meant rationing every commodity and dreading every telegram, for it might bring word that a loved one had become a casualty.

At the end of the War in 1945, things that had been delayed, deferred, or denied became both popular and possible. Basic natural resources that had been diverted to the war effort were becoming available for consumers. The GI Bill offered veterans and their families the chance to buy a home, seek higher education, and get life insurance. Products that had seemed either unaffordable or unavailable became possibilities. New items, like automobiles and appliances and television sets, were soon considered necessities for most households. The baby boom sent a tremor through northeastern Pennsylvania. Seats in the classrooms of public and parochial schools were filled. Churches were crowded too. In the wake of worldwide Depression and the war, the future seemed bright.

Few recognized that these were temporary circumstances. The population data show that Luzerne County had 441,518 residents in the 1940 census. However, fifty years later, the 1990 census reported the population of the county was 328,149, a decline of 26 percent. Specific parts of Luzerne County around Alden suffered even steeper declines.

Nanticoke, which was home to 27,000 residents during the 1930s, began a steady downward trend in population that has seemed irreversible. In the 1970 census, the city counted a population of 14,638 residents. In 1990, it had decreased to 12,267. In 2010, it had further decreased to 10,465. From its peak on the eve of World War II to the most recent census data available, the population of Nanticoke decreased 61 percent.[10] With fewer people, the infrastructure declined. The commercial retail district of Nanticoke virtually disappeared. Churches shrank and closed. Where did the people go? More importantly, why did the people go?

Part of the answer is that the population numbers, which were artificially

---

10   "Pennsylvania Population and Housing Unit Counts," The Bureau of the Census, Office of
      Economics and Statistics Information, United States Department of Commerce (Washington,
      DC: United States Department of Commerce), 2010.

high during the baby boom, have to be seen for their subtleties. The census data show that, although the population of Luzerne County declined significantly between 1940 and 1990, the number of housing units rose by 31 percent. Households grew in number but had fewer individuals in residence. Families were smaller. Increasing numbers of persons lived alone. Where a family of five might have gone to church, perhaps a household of one—a widowed older person or a single younger adult—could be the new norm. But the biggest part of the answer to the demographic questions is the economy.

The "sewing factories," as they were locally known and commonly identified, typically operated as relatively small shops that dotted the regional landscape. They might occupy floors above ground level retail or commercial space. Or they might be stand-alone structures. Fabrics, sometimes precut for particular patterns and sizes of dresses or shirts, would be shipped to the sewing factories where unionized workers stitched them into finished garments that were, in turn, shipped back for retail sales.

It was a successful economic model for businesses. And workers' wages, because of the influence exercised by organized labor, fueled a rising middle class.

But sewing factories could be dangerous places to work. Loose threads and fabric dust had to be contained safely, or they could easily become combustible material. Some of the sewing factories, situated on upper floors of buildings with only one interior stairway, might create congestion at a time of danger. In 1911, the Triangle Shirtwaist fire in New York City claimed the lives of 146 women and men in a blaze caused by both factors.[11]

Those dangers were among the reasons that unionization grew. The ILGWU not only pressed for higher wages but also for safer working conditions.

However, the garment industry found, in the second half of the twentieth century, that the clothing manufacturers could find sufficiently skilled labor at a far lower cost in regions of the country that eschewed unions or in other countries that were less fastidious about worker safety. The garment industry in northeastern Pennsylvania faded away.

11   David Von Drehle, *Triangle: The Fire That Changed America* (New York: Atlantic Monthly Press, 2003).

It was the death of the king, though, that truly transformed the region. Coal had lifted the local economy in a reign that lasted for a hundred years. Then the end came. Coal had been pervasive in the community. Nearly everyone in the region had real and direct contact with coal. Nearly every facet of life was touched by coal. Indeed, coal created for the community a common ethos.

Besides the companies that owned the mines and the people who worked in them, there were countless businesses that produced equipment and supplies used by the mines. Nearly every home was heated by burning coal, and many homes had meals prepared on coal burning stoves or in coal burning ovens. Many families ate their "evening" meals at 3:30 or so in the afternoon because the miners who worked the day shift would typically be home around 3:00 when the miners were on vacation.

There were more ways in which coal created a common ethos. The ash residue from coal that was burned in homes could be used to fill potholes on gravel roads, to provide traction when vehicles became stuck on ice in winter, and even to add a little nutrient to backyard gardens in summer. Companies that mined the coal and that moved it on the rails were benefactors that donated land for organizations from children's baseball leagues (for creating playing fields) to Christian churches (for building places of worship).[12]

The benefits of coal mining were readily visible traits of the local ethos. So were the burdensome breathing ailments that afflicted many miners. In the anthracite region, it was called "anthracosilicosis," a subcategory of the lung disorder that has been known as an occupational hazard for thousands of years and that has been named since the late nineteenth century for a condition that results from breathing silica dust. The name "anthracosilicosis" emerged from the specific debilities suffered by workers who mined anthracite. Ordinary people found their own terms to describe the condition. In coal mining regions such as western Pennsylvania and West Virginia, where bituminous coal was mined, it was called "black lung." Everybody

---

12 Church buildings were often constructed on land that was permanently leased, rather than donated. When coal or rail companies died, churches had difficulties in demonstrating that they had a clear title to the land. More than a year after the Newport United Methodist Church was closed, the annual conference that acquired responsibility for the property was still trying to gain control of the right to sell it. The railroad that had granted permission to use the land for a church building had been folded into other corporations. Closing the church was much easier than acquiring the unencumbered legal authority to sell the property.

from the anthracite region in northeastern Pennsylvania knew someone—or lived with someone—who suffered from what was called "miner's asthma."

The ethos of coal means learning to live at the edge of tragedy, in the valley of the shadow of death. Sometimes the death is the outcome of accumulated injuries through the years that affect a miner's limbs and strain his heart. Sometimes the death is the eventual culmination of a slow, chronic, malignant condition that takes the miner's breath away. Sometimes the death is the immediate result of an explosive burst of water, fire, or gas.

Coal mining is not actually the most dangerous occupation in the United States. One analysis says there are probably as many as fifteen kinds of work with a higher rate of fatalities per hundred thousand workers.[13] But when a single industry is as dominant in an area as anthracite was for a century in northeastern Pennsylvania, the impact of its tragedies reverberates through all levels of the society. Families cope with the injuries, illnesses, breathlessness, and fatalities that occur. And the incidents form the lore of life in the community.

Not far from the spot on the hill where the Methodists built their church in Alden was the John J. Pershing Elementary School. On a Saturday night in May 1928, a mine tunnel in the ground beneath the school collapsed.[14] The entire building, along with a car that belonged to the school custodian, disappeared into the mines below. That event left an indelible impression on the minds of everyone, including my mother who attended the school. Had the collapse occurred during a weekday, when the classes were in session, a hundred children would have died.

Investigations revealed that the cause of the collapse was careless mining in the tunnels below ground. Coal companies with mines in the area accepted responsibility for the failure. They funded the construction of a new elementary school on a site that was at the bottom of the hill in Alden, away from any known mining, and hence safer.[15] That all those little children did

13 David Johnson, "The Most Dangerous Jobs in America," *Time*, May 13, 2016.

14 *Times Leader*, Wilkes-Barre, Pennsylvania, July 14, 1928.

15 Heidi Selecky, "Pershing School, Alden," *Newport Township Newsletter*, Winter 2009. The principal of the Pershing School at the time of the collapse was Thomas Roman. He became the principal of the new structure, which was named Kirtland M. Smith in honor of a coal industry leader. Principal Roman was the husband of Esther Roman, who taught children in the Alden Methodist Sunday School. (www.newporttownship.com/Winter_09_Newsletter.pdf).

not die when the ground collapsed beneath the Pershing school was part of the history of the region. But so were the deaths of many whose lives on earth ended with a tragedy in the mines.

There were multiple dangers. Rock falls, tunnel collapses, explosions of methane gas, flooding, fire, sparks from manual or mechanized mine equipment that ignited coal dust, and failures of the timbers that provided roof support were among them. According to data reported by the Mine Safety and Health Administration of the federal government, there were 109 incidents that were designated fatal mine disasters in the anthracite region between 1846 and 1959.[16] The statistics show that 1,331 persons were killed in these coal mine catastrophes.

But there is some evidence that the actual death toll was much higher. A single incident involving the largest loss of life occurred on September 6, 1869, in the Luzerne County Borough of Plymouth. Data tables from the Mine Safety and Health Administration show that 110 persons were killed in a fire. Other reports, including published documents from the United States Department of the Interior, Bureau of Mines, calculated 179 fatalities in that single event.[17] The written report from the Mine Safety and Health Administration describes in detail how the disaster occurred: "A wooden breaker constricted [*sic*] over the shaft opening to the underground workings caught on fire. The shaft was the sole means of exit from the mine; consequently, the men working underground were trapped and died of suffocation."

But the report also discusses the ways such mine disasters became politicized.

> Catastrophes of the [*sic*] nature aroused tremendous public in-dignation. One result was the formation of a group known as the Molly Maguires, who raised havoc in the anthracite fields, being charged with the deaths of a large number of mine bosses. Al-though it is doubtful if the Mollys had much effect on improv-ing hazardous conditions, they kept the subject of safety and demonstrated how poor accident experience could be made an excuse for mob violence.

---

16   District 1, Fatality Information, Mine Safety and Health Administration Library, Denver, Colorado.

17   James J. Corrigary, in "The Great Disaster At Avondale Colliery, September 6, 1969," Mine Safety and Health Administration, MSHA Library, Denver, Colorado. While the date of this report is not precisely clear, its internal evidence shows that it was released at some point after 1946, probably around 1950.

Obviously, it was not only the Molly Maguires[18] and those seeking to unionize the miners who engaged in political interpretations of tragic events. The mine owners and the mine bosses politicized things from their perspectives as well.

In the middle of all this were the people who worked in the mines, their families, their community organizations, and their churches. They were the ones who lived daily in the valley of the shadow of death. Anecdotes abound with descriptions of mine workers who, under instructions from their bosses, took the body of a colleague who was killed on the job to his home and laid the corpse on the kitchen table—where the widow, perhaps her children, and the rest of her extended family would have to deal with it. The preacher and the undertaker were the professionals to whom they could turn. The church was the community that surrounded the grieving family, nurtured them with food, strengthened them through prayer, and supported others like them with dedication to the principles of collective bargaining in search of better benefits and safer working conditions.[19]

Coal quickly became king in northeastern Pennsylvania in the nineteenth century. Its reign lasted for more than a hundred years. Then, rather abruptly, it ended. And the end came not with a whimper, but a bang.

In compiling its report of the Fatal Mine Disasters in the Anthracite Region, the last one the Mine Safety and Health Administration listed was at the River Slope Mine in the Luzerne County town of Port Griffith. That event, which was—and is—better known in the region as "the Knox Mine Disaster," occurred on January 22, 1959.

On that day, miners were working in a tunnel beneath the Susquehanna River. The weather in the region, which had been extremely cold, quickly warmed and gave way to a January thaw. Huge chunks of ice floated in the river, and its level rose. Suddenly, water and ice broke through the roof of the mine. Twelve miners were trapped in the underground flood.

18   The Molly Maguires or Mollys operated as an Irish-American activist movement that sought improved working conditions for miners. It functioned primarily in the anthracite region, notably in Luzerne County during the late nineteenth century. It was investigated by the Pinkerton agency and opposed by corporate leaders of the coal and rail industries.

19   The Methodist Federation for Social Service, which advocated such efforts, and the Methodist Social Creed, which articulated a theological and ethical rationale for those efforts, were among the church's witness.

Their bodies were never found. The efforts to plug the hole in the riverbed lasted nearly three days and involved pouring enormous quantities of materials from a hillside along the riverbank into the swirling eddy of the stream. In the end, the flood was stopped when immense railcars were rolled on tracks over the hillside and into the swirl. Some of the gondolas actually disappeared into the water, as it rushed through the hole in the riverbed into the mine tunnel before the hole was sealed. By then, perhaps ten billion gallons of water had flowed into the mines underground. Tunnels and shafts and chambers were permanently flooded. Extracting anthracite from the deep mines in Luzerne County ended that day.

Thirteen years later, in June of 1972, a hurricane named Agnes made landfall on the mid-Atlantic coast of the United States. The storm followed a path that covered much of the Susquehanna River valley and dumped huge quantities of rain on Luzerne County. Then, after moving northward, it looped around, made a second run up the river valley, and dumped more rain on the county. The Susquehanna River rose above its banks and, in places, broke through the levees that had been built to strengthen those banks. At its crest, the river was six feet higher than had been previously recorded. Businesses and residences were inundated. Some of the businesses never reopened. Some that did reopen never really recovered.

The Alden United Methodist Church, as it was then known in 1972, was far too high on a hill and much too far from the river to be affected immediately or directly. But indirect impacts were enormous. Population declines remained the prevailing trend, and economic patterns weakened. Retail businesses in the city of Wilkes-Barre closed, and churches did as well. The trend became unalterable.

When the Newport United Methodist Church was euthanized in June 2016, it was the conclusion of a situation that had been developing for decades. It was a long, chronic, malignant process that affected the quality of life in the region and the quantity of people who reside there. In the judgment of the annual conference, a critical mass necessary for church life no longer existed at the site. So it was put to death.

JUDGMENT

When a local church is declared dead, in a community that appears to be dying, and the declaration is by a denomination that may be dying, our faith faces challenges. Can we find words to speak of the situation as a matter of death *and* life?

All the evidence points to the power of death. What standards of judgment allow us to know, by faith, if life has overcome death? What standards of judgment can help us assess the forms of the church that will endure to the end of time? More to the point, what standards of judgment should be used to decide whether The United Methodist Church is too broken to do anything other than euthanize itself?

Practices of ministry and medicine have mutually benefited each other in many ways. In the Gospels, Jesus engaged in the healing arts. In the church, Christians have for about fifteen centuries built health-care institutions. In its mission, Methodism has sent medical missionaries across continents and made health care one of our most prominent public ministries. Hospitals called "Methodist" are widely dispersed, and some are still directly connected to the church. Health-care institutions have pastors and theological scholars on their ethics panels. United Methodist theological schools within universities, and others that formed partnerships with universities, have alliances with research and training programs in schools of medicine and public health. Clinical Pastoral Education (CPE) programs tie theological education to physical health care and mental health care.

One United Methodist theological school, namely Perkins School of Theology at Southern Methodist University, designed its field education courses on models of medical internships. The school calls it an "Intern Program" and requires it as a means to prepare women and men for faithful leadership in Christian ministry.

Perhaps there is something else the church can learn from health practitioners. Since the early years of the twentieth century, a standard facet of medical practice has been a peer review process that involves "mortality and morbidity" conferences. The conferences examine specific cases to discern whether an error (or errors) in professional judgment may have led to the suffering, or possibly to the death, of a patient. The goal of this candid process is to see whether corrections could be made in the future to avoid any painful or possibly fatal complications. It is not about malpractice but about the difficult and mysterious judgments that must regularly be made while performing arts of healing.

Church leaders and theological educators could learn something from these health-care professional practices. We could look honestly at the harsh realities of suffering and dying churches. We could examine circumstances where a church death has occurred and where the power of death appears to prevail. We could allow ourselves enough freedom to recognize mistakes, to reach judgments about them, and to learn from our errors in dealing with the presence and power of death.

When an individual or an institution dies, respect for the one we remember should impel us to know why the life ended. It should prompt us to ask whether something could have been done to ease the pain, if not to prevent an untimely demise altogether. We should study cases of death to learn about life. As part of the process, we will have to allow for the possibility that our own failures contributed to the deadly outcome. But to do that requires taking a risk. We would have to face and confess things that we did (but ought not to have done) and things that we neglected to do (but should have done). We would have to confess our mistakes.[20]

If Methodists were to conduct something akin to these mortality and morbidity conferences, we would have to look carefully at programs that faltered, initiatives that foundered, and ministries that failed, wherever people (whom we intended to serve) sadly suffered, and whenever institutions (founded by the church's belief in the triumph of life) died. We may have to acknowledge something we did wrong or something we neglected to do right. Then perhaps we could find the means to correct our correctible errors.

Churches love to celebrate successes. We highlight "vital" churches. The United Methodist Church created a program called "vital congregations and faithful disciples." And for decades, United Methodists have been infatuated with congregations that seem effective based on the standards that we are using to judge them. We have always kept statistics. So we examine the data for increases in membership, attendance, and finances. Then we celebrate the congregations with the most impressive numbers, pronounce them to be effective, judge them to be successful, and look to them as leaders. We tell their stories, offer conferences where others can learn from their techniques, construct methods for emulating them as models of success, and try to replicate them elsewhere.

Such means of judgment are based on quantitative assessments. They

20 Henry Petroski, *Success Through Failure: The Paradox of Design* (Princeton: Princeton University Press, 2006), 3.

measure things that are readily measurable—how many members are on the rolls, how much money flows through the budget, and how many people make their way to worship. Yet there are flaws in using these quantitative standards for judgment.

One problem lies in trusting that the things we measure are the things that matter. It presumes that quantitative information is directly related to qualitative discipleship. It assumes that there is a direct, positive correlation between those quantities that can be counted and the qualities that are consistent with mission. It celebrates certain statistics as signs of spiritual achievement. This runs the risk that church practices will be skewed toward whatever swells the rolls and sustains the revenues. Do increases in membership and money necessarily imply that the church is focused on its theological mission and on the members' spiritual disciplines?

Another problem is the filter through which church data are examined for internal information (e.g., worship attendance, membership, and money) without also filtering the data for the influence of factors that are external to mission. Churches can grow because real estate and the job market in an area are strong. Churches can grow wherever fear is dominant. Churches can grow if their worship imitates what is socially entertaining even if it is spiritually empty.

Journalist David Gregory went to Joel Osteen's Lakewood Church in Houston, and he reached this judgment about what he experienced: "It can only be described as a show."[21] Then he added another's judgment: "Michael Cromartie, of the Ethics and Public Policy Center, compares Osteen's message to a Twinkie—it goes down easily, he says, but is light on substance and will eventually stunt your growth."[22]

Obviously, Osteen is not a United Methodist. Yet the denomination has made his books available for sale during annual conferences, suggesting that his methods and his message are suitable for Methodist consumption. Is this an indication that his techniques for drawing crowds are consistent with a Wesleyan mission?

Without a filter for all of the external factors that can influence a

---

21 David Gregory, *How's Your Faith? An Unlikely Spiritual Journey* (New York: Simon and Schuster, 2015), 93.

22 Ibid., 217.

congregation or conference or connection, churches become passive recipients of whatever the political, social, ethnic, economic, environmental,
and entertaining options in a region offer. It may not be easy to know if
growth comes from faithful discipleship or false doctrine.

A church in the Wesleyan tradition cannot and should not separate itself
from the culture or the community that it serves. But it cannot and should not
surrender to those circumstances or be victimized by them. It must have a
filter of faith. With a message of death and life, the church must participate
in deciding the directions that the community will take, exercise a vibrant
voice in the choices the community will make, and filter out the other forces
that are theologically fake.

Still another problem with using only quantitative standards for judgment
is a misleading image that may be created by drawing data in momentary
snapshots from which to judge church effectiveness. The Christian Church
in general and the churches of Methodism in particular are organisms living
through time. Current data about Methodism in America cannot be separated from slavery, segregation, and a host of other sociopolitical systems and
secular forces that forged church identity through the centuries. The church
is always in the midst of its living missionary journey. Qualities of commitment
to faith cannot be measured quantitatively in selected episodes or solitary
moments. Judgments about the church need the nuances of theological and
historical insight to frame the data. Numbers alone cannot tell a story unless
they are interpreted. Besides, the data are themselves often debated.

A Gallup poll in 1990 estimated that 40 percent of the American people attended some form of weekly worship. But a team of scholars (Mark
Chaves, Penny Long Marler, and Kirk Hadaway) adapted an "advanced
demographic analysis" and estimated that the real rate of participation in
weekly worship is 20 percent of Americans.[23] The Pew Research Center, in
another report, estimates that the rate of weekly worship attendance is 36
percent for all Americans and 19 percent for Jews in America.[24]

---

23 Kenneth A. Briggs, *The Invisible Best Seller: Searching for the Bible in America* (Grand Rap-
    ids: Eerdmans, 2016), 16.

24 A rate of 10 percent of Jews attend worship on a weekly basis, according to data
    cited by David Gregory in *How's Your Faith*, 135. The Pew Research Center Religion &
    Public Life, however, reports in its *Religious Landscape Study* that the rates of those
    who attend worship each week are larger than the data Gregory cites (www.pew
    forum.org).

A great many Americans hold the view that their nation was founded on the basis of spiritual principles by devout leaders who sought a system of government that could serve a deeply religious constituency. Yet historians believe "only 15% of the colonists belonged to churches" at the time of America's war for independence.[25]

Even supposedly objective data can be disputed. And all data must be interpreted. If a local church has a 5 percent growth in membership and worship attendance during a five-year period, that could be a sign of ecclesial vitality. But if the population in the region has grown 10 percent during that period, then the church is actually declining even though it may cite data that show it is growing. Despite increases in numbers, it is apparently not succeeding in its mission but failing merely to keep pace with local population growth.

The most significant problem in using quantitative standards for judgment is that the church is not being evaluated by factors that actually constitute church identity. It is true that churches are social organizations whose members meet, but they are not merely social organizations with rosters of members. It is true that churches order their activities under leaders they choose through the processes of their polities, but they are not merely political organizations for assigning power and bestowing prestige. It is true that churches need revenue in order to function, but they are not merely revenue-generating businesses. From time to time, churches confuse themselves about such judgments.

A United Methodist pastor confided in me that he was deeply frustrated with his experience during a recent charge conference. His appointment is in the seat of a rural county, where he serves a local church with a few hundred members. The region has a high rate of poverty, and United Methodists in the pastoral charge decided that a major element in their mission was to feed the people living at or near the poverty line. Driven by that missional commitment, they served meals to any persons who came, and they delivered boxes of food to residents in the community.

They tallied the data for their missionary endeavor, and they were ready to report to their charge conference that they had distributed forty thousand pounds of food in one year to their neighbors. The district

25   Briggs, *The Invisible Best Seller,* 15.

superintendent, presiding at their charge conference, acknowledged the pastor's report, which celebrated this food program. But the superintendent showed little eagerness to hear others' reports about it or enthusiasm for it. Instead, the superintendent turned to the main items on his charge conference agenda: worship attendance, membership numbers, and money. The pastor and members of the charge conference were confused and bewildered about whether their commitment to feed the poor and hungry had been supplanted by other definitions of discipleship.

To reach a judgment about matters of death and life, we need to filter the things that are extrinsic to the center of the gospel and focus on the mission of the church. We need to judge which quantitative data are material to the message and mission. And we need to interpret those data through the story of death and life at the heart of the gospel. Telling the story is the way we share the good news. As Daniel Kahneman said, "No one ever made a decision because of a number. They need a story."[26]

So it is important to tell the story of Methodism in northeastern Pennsylvania and to examine it as a case study in failure as part of the larger saga of Methodism. The death of one congregation may yield insight into the sufferings that could be eased and into the death that can be overcome by life through faithful attention to the message of the gospel.

But an objective analysis must come to a fair judgment. Did the little church in Alden die because so much of its economic base was built upon king coal and affiliated industries that had thrived and then disappeared? Did it die because the end of the anthracite mining industry created a climate of failure from which the church could not escape? Did it die because steep population declines made its endurance untenable?

Or did it die because small churches in small towns with big problems had fallen off the radar of Methodist mission? Did it die because the "connection" no longer matters as much to Methodism as the "congregation"? Did it die because United Methodism has let its commitment to the process of salvation atrophy? Did it die because United Methodism in the United States forgot its history of welcoming immigrants? Did it die because United

26 David Leonhardt, review of *The Undoing Project: A Friendship That Changed Our Minds*, by Michael Lewis, *New York Times Book Review*, December 18, 2016, p. 15. See also Daniel Kahneman, *Thinking, Fast and Slow* (New York: Farrar, Straus and Giroux, 2011), especially chap. 36, "Life as a Story."

Methodists have been focusing on local churches becoming big while letting the story of death and life become too small?

A REGION IN THE MIDST OF DEATH AND LIFE

Meanwhile, any judgment about Methodism in northeastern Pennsylvania has to consider the way that the region is gaining some national prominence. Luzerne County (along with its county seat, Wilkes-Barre) and neighboring Lackawanna County (along with its county seat, Scranton) have been receiving increased attention in recent years. Politicians, sociologists, and even criminologists are paying attention to the area.

Politically, the region gained a lot of attention during the election campaigns in 2016. Pennsylvania was recognized as an important swing state in presidential politics. Many journalists from the national news media, both electronic and print, visited voters in northeastern Pennsylvania. So did the major party candidates. Solid majorities of the counties' voters in 2008 and 2012 had supported Barack Obama for the presidency. His margin of victory in 2012 was 5 percent. However, regional voters went in a different direction in 2016. Donald Trump won Luzerne County by 20 percent. Many of his supporters expressed hope that he will bring some changes for the benefit of the middle class, restore good jobs, and perhaps revive the coal industry.

Trump carried the county and the commonwealth. Pennsylvania's electoral votes were decisive in his being victorious. Specifically, the people in the smaller towns across the state voted in greater numbers and switched their allegiance to the Trump candidacy in greater proportions than most of the media anticipated. Professional journalists as well as professional politicians were surprised by the degree to which these changes in voting patterns in smaller communities proved stronger than the voter turnout in larger cities.

Sociologically, the region had been called a "depressed area" for decades. As long ago as the 1960 presidential campaign, candidates Nixon and Kennedy named it in one of their televised debates as a depressed area. Apparently it was considered a very unhappy place as far back as 1940, when attitudinal studies began. For a long time, local residents have been heard to say that the biggest exports from northeastern Pennsylvania were the graduates of local high schools. People have been leaving to pursue better opportunities elsewhere.

Unhappiness seems to be a chronic condition in the area. It has co-existed with decades of economic decline. No one is quite sure whether economic declines generate social unhappiness or whether a condition of social unhappiness lays the groundwork to enervate communities and to lead them into decline. In any case, in 2014, two professors, Joshua Gottlieb and Edward Glaeser, published results of an investigation that found the Wilkes-Barre/Scranton area to be the unhappiest place in the country.[27]

Culturally, this deep sense of distress is manifesting itself in many ways. One is a pervasive drug culture. It has fostered a significant substance abuse problem that has existed for decades but has increased in severity during recent years. Currently, the drugs of choice are heroin and Fentanyl. But methamphetamines and LSD are also widely used. What has become truly frightening in the second decade of the twenty-first century is the dramatic rise in deaths from drug overdoses. The Luzerne County coroner identified 137 deaths by drug overdoses in 2015, and he estimated that drug overdoses claimed 150 lives in 2016. These are the kinds of annual numbers formerly associated with fatal coal mine disasters in the county. The death rate from drug overdoses in Luzerne County today is four times higher than the fatal overdose rate in New York City.[28]

Spiritually, there has been no serious effort to study these conditions or to reach judgments about the ways churches might address them. The working assumption seems to be that declining populations, deteriorating social conditions, and depressing cultural norms lead inevitably to dying churches.

This is true not only for United Methodists. Other Protestant denominations have faced the same grim circumstances. A few independent evangelical bodies have planted churches in the region. But Roman Catholic parishes in northeastern Pennsylvania have either been merged or closed by the diocese.

---

27 Brendan Gibbons, "Study: Scranton, Wilkes-Barre No. 1 in Unhappiness," *The Times Tribune,* July 25, 2014. Glaeser (who is the Fred and Eleanor Glimp Professor of Economics at Harvard) and Gottlieb (an assistant professor at the Vancouver School of Economics in British Columbia) reviewed the data from a survey of three hundred thousand Americans on the question, "How satisfied are you with your life?" Also Shannon M. Monnat, Assistant Professor of Rural Sociology and Demography, Penn State University, in interviews on NPR (December 17, 2016) and CNN (February 25, 2017), expressed similar judgments.

28 Corky Siemaszko, "Wilkes-Barre Faces Heroin Scourge," *NBC News Special Report,* January 9, 2017.

There have been no systematic efforts to study these failures. Hence, no careful judgments have yet been made. The general assumption seems to be that a congregation or parish can only continue to exist in a community as long as financial resources exist to sustain its property and as long as enough members remain on the active rolls to sustain its ministries.

Are United Methodists only connecting to places where local churches prosper? In the middle of the 1990s, Justo Gonzalez compared the way United Methodism reaches its judgments about its ministries to the way a major fast food company makes decisions about its business. He observed that before KFC settles on a site for a new restaurant, it does not ask whether people in that area like chicken, or need chicken, but whether they can afford chicken. In his judgment, the denomination no longer asks if people in an area need Methodism or like Methodism but if they can afford Methodism.[29]

What has been happening across the denomination in recent decades lends some credence to this critique. Many local churches, having decided that they cannot afford full-time ordained ministers, ask their district superintendent for a pastor whose salary and benefit package will be less costly. Many annual conferences, having decided that they cannot afford as many district superintendents as they once appointed to oversee regional ministries, have fewer districts. The district superintendents, facing enlarged geographical territory within the boundaries of their districts, delegate some duties to other persons. Conferences and congregations, having decided that their financial and spiritual resources are too meager to manage emerging challenges, stop wherever they are in their missionary journey and surrender rather than serve. That allows the final word to be a matter of death, not life.

These circumstances can carry profound significance theologically. The message of the gospel goes missing. The resources of the faith are squandered. The triumph of life over death falls silent. And the people whom the church might reach with good news are left to become orphaned children of God.

When ecclesial decisions are made on a basis of affordability and not

---

29 Justo Gonzalez, "Hispanic United Methodists and American Culture," *The People(s) Called Methodist: Forms and Reforms of Their Life* (Nashville: Abingdon, 1997), 241–53.

on the basis of mission, the people in the community of faith and in the community at large are treated like consumers. Churches focus on finding enough customers to cover institutional costs. That makes ministry a matter of satisfying customers and making them feel comfortable.

If connectional values cease to be a missional priority, each congregation can do what it judges to be right in its own eyes.[30] Under these conditions, the gospel may get contorted into whatever the customers are willing to hear and to support, rather than what the ministers of the gospel are called to preach faithfully and forcefully.

When that point is reached, the church has severed its institutional structures from its theological base and has separated its operational activities from its missional identity. It may be premature to make a judgment that United Methodism has reached such a point. But in the absence of a conference on the mortality and morbidity in the case of northeastern Pennsylvania, only hypotheses—not judgments—are possible regarding the church in that region, let alone the denomination as a whole.

If spiritual and theological judgments have not yet been made about Methodism in northeastern Pennsylvania, other assessments have been conducted. And they may point to the spiritual opportunities that exist for telling the story of death and life. Economic journalist Adam Davidson, for example, has examined the departure of major manufacturing employers in the region. He has calculated the loss of jobs in those businesses that once made shoes, garments, and televisions.

> Despite all this, Luzerne County is actually not a deeply depressed area. Its economy has grown modestly over the past decade. Luzerne [County]'s fastest-growing industry, one in which it ranks 13th in the country, is warehousing and storage—an industry driven largely by trade. . . . Wilkes-Barre even has a modest high-tech scene.[31]

So, in looking at the bigger picture, he sees a potentially brighter future for the region. However, as Davidson notes, "newly arrived Latino workers" take most of the jobs in warehouses and young college graduates take most of the technology jobs. It is going to be a time of significant transition

---

30 Judges 17:6, 21:25; Proverbs 21:2.

31 Adam Davidson, "On Money," *New York Times Magazine*, July 10, 2016.

for the area. Some citizens, imagining that former patterns of mining and manufacturing will return, are going to be disappointed. And many Methodists, hoping that members and money will return, are probably still clinging to the forces of death rather than to the promise of life.

Methodists will tell the story of death and life only if we can find the missionary motivation to reach newer groups of immigrants and newer generations of residents. In a setting that a century ago devoted itself to serving an immigrant constituency, new waves of immigrants must be reached. In a setting that a century ago devoted itself to addressing substance abuse by alcohol, church leaders will have to find the means to minister where a different lethal drug problem exists.

In a denomination that a century ago began to emphasize its local churches and to let its connection erode, there is much to be done. The connection needs rebirth. These are matters of death and life. And all of this has to be faced while the denomination is choosing whether to live or to die.

QUESTIONS FOR DISCUSSION

1. How would you describe the community where you were raised?

   • Was it a small town, a neighborhood in a big city, a rural area, a small city?

   • Did it have ethnic, linguistic, or racial diversity?

   • Were you raised near members of your extended family?

   • What types of religious groups were present in the region?

2. Were you raised with a church affiliation?

3. Whether or not you were raised in a church:

   • Can you recall how your local community viewed the church?

   • What memories from childhood and youth do you associate with the church?

   • Who were your mentors or teachers in the church or community?

   • Were there any pastors whom you particularly remember?

      — In what ways was she/he especially significant or influential in your life?

- Where or with whom did she/he have the greatest impact:
    — Upon individuals?
    — Within the congregation?
    — In the community?

4. Who are the most significant religious leaders currently?

- What are their major contributions?
- Is their influence mainly with one generation or group?

5. Have you ever been affiliated with a local church that closed?

PART THREE

DIVISION

Forgive, O Lord,
The souls of all the faithful departed
From all the chains of their sins
And by the aid to them of your grace
May they deserve to avoid the judgment of revenge
And enjoy the blessedness of everlasting light.

Tract following *Kyrie Eleison* from *Requiem*

RATIONALES

"The Bible hardly ever discusses homosexual behavior. There are perhaps half a dozen references to it in all of scripture. In terms of emphasis, it is a minor concern, in contrast, for example, to economic injustice.... Would that the passion presently being expended in the church over the question of homosexuality were devoted instead to urging the wealthy to share with the poor!" (Richard B. Hays)[1]

"I don't think God is done with me yet.... I've signed away my right to live out my calling—to be most fully who God has called me to be—I hope only for a time. My heart is broken, yet I trust that God will work through even this for good.... I think we have to realize that there could come a time when staying [in the denomination] may not be healthy. That it may be better to make a change." (Rev. Cynthia Meyer)[2]

"There's going to be a better day for faithful United Methodists, whether we're able to hold this Church together, whether we're able to step into a place of vibrant Wesleyan orthodoxy within this denomination—which I am still bold enough to pray for—or whether there is going to have to be some kind of separation that will set evangelical, orthodox, Wesleyan believers free to pursue a missionary Church that is committed to converting people to the truth of Jesus Christ." (Rev. Rob Renfroe)[3]

SCHEMES FOR SCHISM

Will The United Methodist Church die fifty years after it began? Will the denomination disappear in division? Will it euthanize itself as an institution? Will it do so because of disunity over homosexuality?

---

1   Richard B. Hays, "Awaiting the Redemption of Our Bodies: The Witness of Scripture Concerning Homosexuality," in *Homosexuality in the Church: Both Sides of the Debate*, ed. Jeffrey S. Siker (Louisville: Westminster John Knox, 1994), 5.

2   Rev. Cynthia Meyer, quoted in Donald Bradley, "Gay Pastor Agrees to Leave Her Post at Johnson County Church," *Kansas City Star*, August 18, 2016. The article was published after Rev. Meyer agreed to begin an involuntary leave of absence from pastoral ministry rather than face a church trial.

3   Rev. Rob Renfroe, quoted in Becca Andrews, "The Methodist Church May Split Over LGBT Issues," *Mother Jones*, August 29, 2016. The article quotes remarks by Rev. Renfroe, the president of *Good News*, after the election of Rev. Dr. Karen Oliveto as a bishop of The United Methodist Church by the Western Jurisdictional Conference on July 15, 2016.

Methodists through the years have attempted to list behaviors that are enough to disqualify a person from being a disciple of Jesus. Most often, they have been matters of personal conduct and individual discipline. In the late nineteenth and early twentieth centuries, for example, denominational laws prohibited dancing, attending theaters, going to circuses,[4] and "drinking spirituous liquors, unless in cases of necessity."[5] Until 1968, the use of tobacco or the consumption of beverage alcohol was enough to preclude someone from being (or from remaining) an ordained minister of the church.[6] The General Conference passed church laws about such things; then annual conferences and individual Methodists honored them, ignored them, or used them to critique neighbors who failed to heed them.

Occasionally, the proscribed behaviors have been systemic, not simply personal. Some led to separation or schism. The Wesleyan Church became a separate denomination over the issue of slavery in 1843. In the following year, the Methodist Episcopal Church in the United States of America divided into two major regional churches when it was not able to resolve a dispute over the question of whether someone could simultaneously be a slave owner and a Methodist bishop.

In recent decades, indeed for most of its existence as a denomination, The United Methodist Church has focused its exclusionary attention on homosexuality. With growing rigor, the church has written laws about sexual boundaries within which heterosexual and homosexual persons must live. If not, they can be expelled, exiled, or excluded.

Complaints have been filed against clergy, including bishops, alleging violations of those laws. Some accused clergy have been placed on leave or have been suspended while the complaints against them were

---

4   *The Doctrines and Discipline of The Methodist Episcopal Church 1892*, ed. Bishop Edward G. Andrews, (New York: Hunt and Eaton), ¶ 240.

5   *The Doctrines and Discipline of The Methodist Episcopal Church, South, 1894*, ed. J. Tigert (Nashville: Publishing House of the M. E. Church, South), ¶ 28.

6   The last appearance of this legislation is in *Doctrines and Discipline of The Methodist Church, 1964*, ed. Emory Stevens Bucke (Nashville: The Methodist Publishing House), ¶¶ 306.6 and 322.5(5). These ecclesial laws were enforced differently in different regions. In some annual conferences, such as those within the states of North Carolina and Kentucky, church laws regarding the use of tobacco were ignored, overlooked, or simply not enforced. After the removal of the ban on tobacco and alcohol use by clergy in 1968, many United Methodists tried to reinstate its designation as a prohibited practice, but they were unsuccessful. (See Judicial Council Decisions 316 and 318.)

processed. Some have been tried, convicted, and sentenced. Some have been successful in appealing their convictions or sentences. And some have withdrawn from ordained ministry in The United Methodist Church, found opportunities in other denominations, or left the pastoral ministry altogether.

For the moment, the church has remained institutionally whole and un-broken by a separation or schism over these matters. Complaints against clergy who are alleged to be in violation of church laws get attention. So do cases where congregations announce their intentions to separate from the denomination. The relevant bodies of the church—in most situations, annual conferences—handle such things according to ecclesiastical law.

Yet on the matter of homosexuality, the risks to institutional church unity are as apparent as the fissures in the Antarctic ice sheet. And the disputants on opposing sides of the chasm are almost as rigidly frozen in their positions.

Among the matters that the denomination's laws and official policies leave unsettled is whether one's sexual orientation is a structural component of being human or a moral choice a person makes. One official text, within the Social Principles of The United Methodist Church, affirms that sexuality is "God's good gift to all persons," that it is a "sacred gift," and that "all persons are sexual beings, whether they are married or not." To that, the church adds, "All persons are individuals of sacred worth," regardless of their sexual orientation. Yet the same text in the Social Principles also says that only heterosexual persons may express their "sacred worth" sexually and that they must do so within "the covenant of monogamous, heterosexual marriage."[7] In other words, no matter how one is created sexually, a United Methodist must function sexually in a certain way or one may not function sexually at all, according to church policy.

Technically, individuals who engage in homosexual practices are wel-come in the church. But any pastor can prohibit practicing homosexuals from membership in a local church.[8] All practicing homosexuals are officially stigmatized by their conduct, which is "incompatible with Christian teaching" according to church law and social policy.[9] The ordained ministry is closed

---

7   "Social Principles: II, The Nurturing Community," in *The Book of Discipline of The United Meth-odist Church 2016* ¶ 161 G, pp. 112–13. It is far more important and significant that the phrase "sacred worth" also is part of the Constitution of The United Methodist Church (see ¶ 4, p. 26).

8   See Decision 1032 by the Judicial Council of The United Methodist Church.

9   See *The Book of Discipline of The United Methodist Church 2016*, ¶ 161 G and ¶ 304.3, pp. 113, 226.

to homosexual persons, unless they cease sexual activities and commit to lives of celibacy, knowing that any violation of their chastity would risk removal from the ranks of the ordained. Further, any ordained minister who conducts a marriage ritual for a gay couple runs the same risk of facing a complaint, with the possibility of dismissal from clergy orders.[10]

Writing religious laws to constrain sexual activity is hardly new terrain. Leviticus has plenty of such legislation in its holiness code,[11] although most of it is concerned with heterosexual behavior. Disobedience could mean punishment, banishment, or death. The author of 1 Timothy (who may or may not have been Paul) seems to have had a fondness for church laws, including those on sexual activity, but wants all laws used "legitimately."[12]

In Romans, 1 Corinthians, and other letters that are universally accepted as Paul's own writing, the apostle offers what might be described as evangelical recommendations for Christian behavior. But Paul is quite reticent about writing ecclesiastical legislation. Even when he warns against troublemakers, like the "dogs" and the "evil workers" whom he sees as enemies of the gospel, Paul celebrates "not having a righteousness of my own that comes from the law, but one that comes through faith in Christ."[13] He certainly lets readers infer that laws (even laws about sexual activities) offer no path to salvation.

In the few New Testament passages that refer to homosexuality, none calls for schism. Paul threatens miscreants of many kinds with eternal damnation,[14] yet he warns against "passing judgment on another." So the biblical support one can find for writing rules that condemn certain sexual behaviors may not support separation.

To complicate things for United Methodists, there is one place in the documents that order the life of the church where one's sexual identity, if not one's sexual activity, is protected rather than outlawed. What's more,

---

10   Ibid., ¶¶ 340.2(a)(3)(a) and 2702.1, pp. 275, 788–89.

11   See especially Leviticus 18:6–23, 19:20–22, and 20:10–21.

12   1 Timothy 1:8–11.

13   Philippians 3:2, 9.

14   See Romans 1:29–2:1. It should be noted that the list of miscreants whose behaviors are condemned in the epistles is not limited to those who engage in what are perceived to be sexual improprieties. None of the "greedy," for instance, "will inherit the kingdom of God," according to 1 Corinthians 6:10.

this protection has *constitutional* authority. In Division One, Article IV, labeled *"Inclusiveness of the Church,"* the Constitution says,

> The United Methodist Church acknowledges that all persons are of sacred worth. All persons without regard to race, color, national origin, status, or economic condition, shall be eligible to attend its worship services, participate in its programs, receive the sacraments, upon baptism be admitted as baptized members, and upon taking vows declaring the Christian faith, become professing local members in any local church in the connection. In The United Methodist Church no conference or other organizational unit of the Church shall be structured so as to exclude any member or any constituent body of the Church because of race, color, national origin, status or economic condition.[15]

This text has an amendment to the Constitution, adopted overwhelmingly by the General Conference in 2000[16] after extended debate and then affirmed by the aggregate votes of the annual conferences. That amendment inserted "sacred worth" into the Constitution. The phrase "sacred worth" has existed within the Social Principles since 1972 as a statement that applies to the identity of homosexual as well as heterosexual persons.[17] The Social Principles are the church's official witness on matters of public discussion and public policy, though they are not church law. However, when a constitutional amendment was approved, it established the phrase "sacred worth" as a constitutional guarantee of protected identity. Because The United Methodist Church now "acknowledges that all persons are of sacred worth" within its Constitution, all matters of church law must be measured against that constitutional standard, including laws about sexual activity.

Eight years earlier, in 1992, a constitutional amendment was adopted by the General Conference and was subsequently affirmed by the aggregated votes of the annual conferences, inserting the word "status" where it now appears in the same Article IV.[18] The word occurs twice, in two sequences of

---

15 See *The Book of Discipline of The United Methodist Church 2016* ¶ 4, p. 26.

16 The vote was 700–170, which means 80 percent of the delegates (far more than the required two-thirds) favored the amendment. See the *Daily Christian Advocate*, May 13, 2000, p. 2452.

17 *The Book of Discipline of The United Methodist Church 1972*, ¶ 72C, p. 86.

18 Following ratification by the annual conferences, the revision appeared for the first time in *The Book of Discipline of The United Methodist Church 1996*, ¶ 4, p. 22.

terms, four of which describe an inherent identity based on one's birth and the other of which ("economic condition") describes a circumstance that is beyond an individual's capacity fully to control by choice. These aspects of human identity are listed in two ways: as traits by which persons are *to be included* in the church, and as traits by which they *cannot be excluded* from the church.

So "race, color, national origin, status, or economic condition" cannot be used as grounds for some separation from the church. Rather, they are constitutionally sufficient markers of identity for inclusion in the church.

But what does the Constitution of The United Methodist Church mean with this reference to the "status" of a person? In the quarter century since the General Conference approved the amendment and sent it to the annual conferences for their votes, the word has never been officially defined. The Judicial Council has been asked repeatedly to give a definitive ruling on the meaning of "status" and has consistently determined that only the General Conference can do so.[19] At last, in 2016, the General Conference approved and sent to the annual conferences a constitutional amendment that would (if approved by two-thirds of the aggregate votes at annual conferences) insert the word "marital" in front of "status" in Article IV of the Constitution. The adjective would modify status and mean that the word "status" is definitively about marriage. The outcome of annual conferences' voting on this proposed constitutional amendment (and others that are also proposed) will not be known until some point in 2018. Whether its adoption would add clarification or confusion to the situation is a matter of debate.

At a superficial level, the phrase "marital status" in the Constitution could simply mean that both married and unmarried persons are welcome in the church. Married and unmarried alike are to be included and cannot be excluded from United Methodist life.

But different cultures and countries have different definitions of marriage. In the United States, the *Obergefell* decision by the Supreme Court in June 2015 declared that homosexual couples have the same marital rights as heterosexual couples. In fifty-eight nations of the world, polygamy is legal. So a phrase in the United Methodist Constitution that guarantees inclusion and prohibits exclusion based on "marital status" might create some

---

19   See, for example, Judicial Council Decision 702.

new controversy without resolving an existing one. Civil laws differ in nations where United Methodism exists.

In any case, the word *status* and the phrase *marital status* refer to ways that human beings identify themselves, not to activities in which they may engage. We can be certain that there are single persons who engage in sexual activities and also that there are married persons who do not engage in sexual activities. The "status" or "marital status" of their lives describes who they are, not what they do.

The United Methodist Church has both a Constitution and a set of laws that are published together in its *Book of Discipline*. But the church's laws are subordinate to the Constitution and must adhere to a standard of constitutionality if put to that test. The use of the word *status* or the phrase *marital status* in the Constitution, like the phase *sacred worth* in the Constitution, shows that The United Methodist Church places a higher authority and higher priority on human identity—who persons are—than on human behavior.

The issue that divided Northern and Southern Methodists in the United States and that created schism in the church in 1844 was not behavior but identity. The dispute that divided the General Conference in 1844 was not whether Bishop James O. Andrew was benevolent and kind or brutal and abusive to his slaves. The reason for schism was a social, political, economic, and legal system, which assigned less than fully human status to some category of human beings. The dispute was whether slaves were persons of sacred worth, though that phrase was not in use at the time. The divisive question was whether the church tolerated a system that enslaved and dehumanized persons.

What divided Methodists was slavery, which allowed human beings to be assigned a status other than that of being "human." It provided—in civil as well as ecclesial law, and in religious as well as economic practice—that people could be treated as property. Methodists divided into separate denominations along boundaries of free and slave states because of a construct called slavery (and its link to a construct called race). They split over a system that created, systemically and systematically, a status that was not fully human.

Tragically, the people called Methodists decided that they could not find unity in the principle that all human beings are created in the image of God. So they separated in 1844. The institutional fracture lasted nearly a hundred years, and its racialized legacy has lasted a lot longer than that. In a relic of that wrongful past, we have this reflection from a nineteenth-century Methodist bishop: "Uncle Cy was the homeborn slave of my grandfather. . . . He obeyed his master. . . . Indeed, our children and the generations following can never know the sentiment that sprang up between the two races under the system of domestic slavery. It had its evil and it had its good. Both are gone forever."[20]

Today, the theological descendants of John Wesley are appalled that a bishop of the church could have imagined any way in which slavery might be considered "good."

Since 1844, much has changed. The American Constitution has been amended, the nation's laws have been changed, and the country's Supreme Court has unanimously ruled that separate is inherently not equal in public education. The church's Constitution has dismantled the racially segregated system of jurisdictions that was designed to preclude race mixing. The United Methodist Church has established, in its Constitution, that "race, color, national origin, status, or economic condition" are signs of inclusion and cannot be reasons for exclusion. And the church, in its Constitution, has acknowledged that "all persons are of sacred worth."

These are the constitutional and the legal standards that unify the church. But is a Constitution with a set of laws (which incorporate retirement programs worth billions of dollars and a trust clause that controls ownership of all church property, for instance) all that can hold The United Methodist Church together?

Even if all United Methodists could agree on the meaning of the terms "sacred worth" and "status" and "incompatible with Christian teaching" in their Constitution and *Discipline*, such agreements could never be the basis on which the unity of the church is built. Methodism seeks to provide *order* for its life through a Constitution and a set of laws. But Methodism has its *identity* elsewhere—in God's grace through Jesus Christ! Grace defines us.

Like most Protestant traditions, Methodism came into being as an alternative to a concept of an established religion or a national church. It had to find and name a reason to exist that did not depend on the political

---

20 Bishop Holland N. McTyeire, "My Old Servant, 'Uncle Cy'" (c. 1868), John James Tigert IV Collection, Vanderbilt University Library.

preference of a monarch or an ideology. It had to develop a means or method to operate that did not rely on political authorities.

In the American context, Methodism found a way to honor its theological identity and its organizational polity. It was unlike the English system (with an established Anglican church that tolerated a variety of dissenting religious bodies) or a Chinese system (which controls religious life under the auspices of the state). American Methodism emerged as a church that operated on its own authority. In 1784, before there was a Constitution of the United States with a Bill of Rights that guaranteed the freedom of religion, the Methodist "conference claimed supremacy for itself," wrote Russell Richey.[21] Ecclesial Methodism took shape in North America as a church that decided for itself how to define itself and how to order itself.

Such churches, according to Craig Dykstra and James Hudnut-Beumler, use three different models: as voluntary societies that form constitutional confederacies; as public corporations that develop "religious bureaucracies"; and as "regulatory agencies" that try to control procedures, policies, and people.[22] But these are church *functions*, not church identity. A constitutional confederacy operates only as long as the confederates honor their constitution. A religious corporation operates only as long as a bureaucracy does business according to the wishes of its stakeholders. A regulatory agency operates only as long as individuals and groups are willing to be regulated. That is how churches *function*.

But that is not who churches *are*. It is not the source of their identity. Churches have to find their unity in their identity. And their identity is not in their constitutions, their disciplined practices, their rules, or their voting majorities. The church finds its identity in the grace of Jesus Christ.

In the gospel, Jesus frames moral misconduct in terms that transcend legislation or regulations. He shrinks the commandments of the law to two imperatives about love.[23] His vivid narratives, like the parable of the good

---

21   Richey, *The Methodist Conference*, 36.

22   "The National Organization Structures of Protestant Denominations: An Invitation to a Conversation," in Milton J. Coalter, John M. Mulder, Louis B. Weeks, eds., *The Organizational Revolution: Presbyterians and American Denominationalism* (Louisville: Westminster John Knox Press, 1992).

23   Matthew 22:36–40; Mark 12:28–34; Luke 10:25–37.

Samaritan, celebrate reconciling love that surpasses religious law.[24] Indeed, Jesus—whose word in the Gospels has nary a note about homosexuality—frames sexual activity in forms that are beyond, beneath, before, and beside restrictive regulations. In his message, even immoral sexual activity cannot be a reason to exclude what the love of God includes. His gospel is not about bad and good behavior. It is about death and life.

Jesus' parable of the prodigal son begins as a tale about someone who is so selfish that he wants his inheritance even before his father dies. In effect, the young man wishes his father were dead and asks to be treated as if his father were dead: "There was a man who had two sons. The younger of them said to his father, 'Father, give me the share of the property that will belong to me.' So he divided his property between them" (Luke 15:11–12).

The story then details his irresponsible and self-destructive behavior, which leads him to abject poverty and unfathomable misery. His circumstances are so wretched that he shares space with swine—the animals that his religious community shuns. So he is a religious exile with no fortune, no family, no faith, no food, no home, and no hope.

In that state, he concocts a possibly deceitful ploy to exploit his father's mercy. "I will get up and go to my father, and I will say to him, 'Father, I have sinned against heaven and before you. I am no longer worthy to be called your son; treat me like one of your hired hands'" (Luke 15:18–19).

But he never gets to play the ploy. The father runs to him. Love overcomes everything.

The story then shifts into details about a divisive family squabble. An older son exhibits jealousy, self-pity, entitlement, bitterness, and anger. He says that the indulgent father has enabled the younger son's disgusting, sinful behavior. He speaks sternly to his father. "Listen! For all these years I have been working like a slave for you, and I have never disobeyed your command. . . . But when this son of yours came back, who has devoured your property with prostitutes, you killed the fatted calf for him" (Luke 15:29–30).

The parable is a story of love, loyalty, financial malfeasance, sexual misconduct, and sibling rivalry. It invokes ancient inheritance laws and matters of religious discipline. But Jesus frames all these issues differently. They are

---

24   Luke 10:29–37.

matters of death and life. He says so, through the words of a loving father. Indeed, Jesus has the father say it twice! "This son of mine was dead and is alive again. . . . This brother of yours was dead and has come to life" (Luke 15:24, 32).

The United Methodist Church is facing the possibility of death, as its debates over homosexuality may lead to division, schism, or institutional dissolution of some kind in the very near future. There are discussions about whether schism has merit, is wise, or may even be "inevitable" as at least one church theologian has asserted.[25] The president of the Council of Bishops, the normally non-hyperbolic Bruce Ough, in his presidential address said that "the entire United Methodist Church is holding its breath" about the possibility of a fracture. The bishops and a commission they have named are wondering how they can lead the denomination without dividing the church.

A climactic decision could occur at a special session of the General Conference in 2019. During February of that year, the delegates may face a choice between two priorities: laws about moral conduct or the gospel of death and life. Perhaps then it will be clear whether the denomination has decided to euthanize itself.

If the feuding forces in the denomination choose to terminate the church by separating The United Methodist Church into parts, how would the schism happen? How might the institutional division actually occur? What form would the divided pieces of the church take?

It is one thing to decide, for reasons of theology or morality, that disputing parties can no longer remain within the same denomination. It is another thing to determine how a separation could be achieved. Moreover, it is immensely challenging to find a form of fracture that lets the broken parts retain stewardship over the assets of the denomination.

The list of such assets is immense. The United Methodist Church has billions of dollars invested in church retirement programs and has obligations to the persons who are covered by the promises made through those programs. The denomination has untallied billions of dollars invested in physical properties: land, buildings, antiquities, historical relics, works of art, and

25   Ted A. Campbell, plenary address to the World Methodist Conference, August 31, 2016, in Houston, Texas.

mineral rights. The denomination also boasts institutions ranging from higher education[26] to health care.[27] And it controls libraries, archives, web domains, copyrights, camps, and conference centers. In addition, it has endowments that are established for specific purposes to fund its institutions, and they must be honored.

Human beings dissolve their relationships all the time. Professional organizations (such as law partnerships and medical practices) divide. Marriages terminate in divorce. Businesses partnerships close.

But the persons at the center of a separation, who may be at an impasse with each other and who may intensely disagree with each other, must find ways to agree on terms for a separation. Without clear agreements, the resources they have accumulated and the assets for which they are responsible may be squandered. Moreover, unless the separating parties are careful, they may be too reckless in their haste to separate. Casual, emotional, or indifferent behavior could lead them to violate the terms of their original unity. They might forfeit their rights in the marital or institutional union that they so eagerly want to leave. It also is possible that, without exercising great care, they might violate civil laws and incur personal or organizational penalties as part of the process. For couples seeking to terminate a marriage and commercial organizations seeking to end a partnership in a business, there are tax implications, for example. Churches do not pay taxes in the United States under most circumstances, but there could be applicable laws involving liens.

If United Methodists decide to sever their relationships with one another, they will have to cut their connecting cords carefully. One way to sever ties to a church is just to leave it. Individual members—clergy and laity—are free to flee from The United Methodist Church whenever they may wish. United Methodism exists as a voluntary association. No one is required to be a member, and no member is required to stay within the church. There are no countries on earth that impose The United Methodist Church as their established religion. The island nation of Tonga has a Methodist Church as an official religion, and Tonga's king is the head of the church. But Tongan Methodism is not within United Methodism.

---

26   The South Central Jurisdictional Conference owns Southern Methodist University.

27   The Texas Annual Conference owns Houston Methodist Hospital and Medical Center.

Wherever United Methodists gather across the globe, they do so by their personal choice. People take vows of membership as individuals. They may renounce their vows and depart from membership as individuals. Any United Methodist can leave freely.

However, each can do so only as a single person departing from membership. No member holds a share of ownership of the church or has any claim on it. No individual or group of individuals can take any of the institution's assets in such a departure.

If a local church in United Methodism has a thousand members and if all of them decide voluntarily to leave that local church and the denomination, they are free to do so. But they leave as individuals, not as a corporate body. They cannot hold a meeting and take an action whereby they seize ownership of church property.[28] They cannot arbitrarily claim that their financial contributions or volunteer efforts through the years grant equity in a corporation or organization. They do not retain any rights to the financial assets, the endowments, or the cash on deposit in the church's bank accounts.

If every individual member of a local church were to leave and if, as a result, an annual conference declares the local church to be "closed,"[29] all of the resources of that local church belong to the annual conference. The departing former members will leave empty-handed, unless they reach a firm agreement on what they are allowed to take with them. If a clergy or lay member wants to exercise a claim — to take a Bible from the premises, for instance — some action will have to occur through an annual conference decision or through negotiation or through litigation to achieve the goal.

There are other issues for United Methodists to consider as they imagine schism. Church separations, at least in the United States of America, have to cope with the country's Constitution. The Bill of Rights could perhaps pose a problem.

---

28 Robin Wilson, *God Is With Us: An Advent Study Based on the Revised Common Lectionary* (Nashville: Abingdon Press, 2016), 33. Dr. Wilson, who is now co-pastor of Dauphin Way United Methodist Church in Mobile, Alabama, describes a small membership church in rural Alabama where she previously served as the pastor. Members of the congregation, who were irate about the civil rights movement and mandates for racial integration, left the denomination, formed a new church, and kept the building. "Years later," she writes, "the state supreme court returned the church building to the rightful congregation."

29 *The Book of Discipline of The United Methodist Church 2016*, ¶ 2549.2(b), p. 771.

Under the First Amendment in the Bill of Rights, the "free exercise" clause gives churches wide latitude to run their own affairs by their own rules. If United Methodists break their church apart, the denomination will have to honor its own rules for dividing. Otherwise, a schism could arouse the ire of some who feel aggrieved by the outcome. A suit could claim the church failed to follow its own rules. Costly and lengthy litigation could follow. When the denomination is pondering division, the church should know its own procedures, practices, and laws that may apply to such a separation.

So, if indeed The United Methodist Church decides to divide according to its own rules, how might it do so? Answers to that question have to begin with acknowledging that, by its odd self-understanding, "The United Methodist Church" *does not exist*. At least, The United Methodist Church does not actually exist as a whole unit under the law. Paragraph 141 of *The Book of Discipline of The United Methodist Church 2016* says that terms or labels, which apply to the denomination (including even its name), refer to the many different forms of a "connectional" character "which collectively constitute the religious system known as United Methodism." Crucially, the text of ¶ 141 then adds the following:

> Under the Constitution and disciplinary procedures set forth in this *Book of Discipline*, "The United Methodist Church" as a denominational whole *is not an entity*, nor does it possess legal capacities and attributes. It does not and cannot hold title to property, nor does it have any officer, agent, employee, office, or location. Conferences, councils, boards, agencies, local churches, and other units bearing the name "United Methodist" are, for the most part, legal entities capable of suing and being sued and possess of legal capacities.[30]

Hence, dividing the denomination would not actually involve breaking apart an entity called "The United Methodist Church." It would involve a realignment of all the numerous elements, which are the connected entities that form the denomination.

Well, how might such realignment happen? There probably are multiple ways for the United Methodist connection to design a schism and to dissolve itself. But all of them are variations of two basic models. One is to "divorce." The other is to "disconnect."

---

30 *The Book of Discipline of The United Methodist Church 2016*, ¶ 141, p. 102 (emphasis added).

DIVORCE

In a "divorce," a wedded couple is split apart. A marriage union dissolves, and from its dissolution two unrelated individuals emerge as separate parties. By agreement or decree, each person becomes the custodian or owner of a share of the assets and the obligations they formerly held together within their union.

If United Methodism were to go through a divorce and if two separate parties were to emerge from the proceedings, they would have to reach an agreement to protect the assets and fulfill the obligations of the predecessor church. Each successor party to an agreement would acquire a portion of the assets and obligations. As in all divorces, there certainly would be shrinkage of the total asset pool. The costs for legal services would be one drain on the assets, and there might be some loss of value in other assets that must be converted to cash quickly for distribution. So a divorce would potentially be costly.

Yet the church certainly could find a method for divorce. In so doing, presumably each of the two groups of feuding antagonists would be happy to be rid of the other.

Assuming that two new denominations would emerge and would be differentiated by their views on homosexuality, they might call themselves "The Orthodox Methodist Church" (OMC) and "The Progressive Methodist Church" (PMC). In the details of the divorce agreement, the separating parties would decide the parts of United Methodism that move into the OMC and the parts that move into the PMC.

In such a divorce, the assets would not necessarily have to stay in their current form when they were divided. The two separating parties could devise structures within constitutions and create sets of laws or disciplines for the new institutions.

For example, United Methodism today includes five regional "jurisdictions" in the United States and seven "central conferences" in other parts of the world.[31] A divorce would have to account for all of the resources

---

31   Just to make things a bit more complicated, the jurisdictions within the United States are named and their boundaries are defined in the Constitution of The United Methodist Church (¶ 37, p. 37). The Constitution does not name the central conferences or define their boundaries, but it delegates that authority to the General Conference (¶ 38, p. 38). Hence the current names and boundaries of central conferences come from legislative acts by the General Conference (¶ 540.3, p. 383) and are not, strictly speaking, constitutional matters.

of these twelve entities, but jurisdictional or central conferences would not need to exist in the new institutions. The duties, roles, responsibilities, and assets of these intermediate level conferences could be assigned to a general conference (or an entity with another name) in each of the two successor bodies.

The details would have to be defined, designed, and drafted. But the foes might agree in 2019 that The United Methodist Church would cease to exist at the end of the day on December 31, 2020, according to Greenwich Mean Time, and that the successor churches (OMC and PMC) would begin to exist on January 1, 2021. They might agree, as well, that entities currently within The United Methodist Church would choose which of the two successor bodies would be their "Methodist" community in the new arrangement.

Under such a plan, each jurisdictional or central conference would meet for a final time in calendar year 2020 and would cease to exist in 2021. By majority vote at the final meeting, each would choose whether to be absorbed by the OMC or the PMC. In making such a decision by majority vote, each jurisdictional or central conference would thus be choosing the body to which all of its assets and obligations would be transferred. Each of the jurisdictional or central conferences would be voting itself out of existence, by terms of the divorce decree. Their assets and obligations would exist but in a different form of alignment.

If a majority of the delegates to the South Central Jurisdictional Conference were to vote in favor of its absorption by the Orthodox Methodist Church, for example, then Southern Methodist University would therefore become part of the Orthodox Methodist Church. Similarly, a central conference (and any of the assets it owns or controls) would by majority vote be absorbed into the OMC or the PMC. Because the jurisdictional and central conferences would cease to exist under such a plan, the votes taken by them would simply determine into which of the two surviving churches (OMC or PMC) they would be immersed and absorbed. That would be a means within the law of the church to deal with the jurisdictional and central conferences in a divorce. They could simply disappear.

But, in this plan, each annual conference and each provisional annual conference would continue to exist in and beyond 2021 through a connection to a successor church. An annual conference is not a subsidiary body or a delegated body. An annual conference is a membership body, and it is "the basic body of the church" according to the Constitution of The United Methodist Church.[32] An annual conference would not need to disappear in a divorce. Rather, at meetings in 2020, each annual conference would select one Methodist body (OMC or PMC) with which it would choose to be connected. Clergy members of the North Georgia Annual Conference would still be clergy members of the North Georgia Annual Conference after a divorce, and members of local churches in that annual conference would still be connected to the North Georgia Annual Conference. But the churches and clergy would all be connected to a different denomination. Clergy whose annual conferences affiliated with the OMC and who wanted to be in an annual conference affiliated with the PMC could seek to transfer conferences. The terms of the divorce would have to be explicit about the relative ease of doing so.[33]

There is precedent for such an action. In 1844, when the Methodist Episcopal Church in the United States of America divided over slavery, the schism was essentially a divorce. Two new church bodies—the Methodist Episcopal Church and the Methodist Episcopal Church, South—were formed by the terms of the separation. Those terms were negotiated when a General Conference of the Methodist Episcopal Church of the United States of America met for the last time.[34] The annual conferences aligned themselves with one or the other of the two new church bodies. At least one bishop chose to affiliate with the southern church rather than with the one in the North, which was his home territory. Individual clergy could transfer to annual conferences in another Methodist church, if they wished.

While the precedent may be useful, the church situation in 1844 did

---

32 See Section VI, Article II, in the Constitution, published as ¶ 33 (pp. 35–36) in *The Book of Discipline of The United Methodist Church 2016*.

33 And the terms of the divorce would have to be drawn with an appreciation for the global nature of the church. Would both the OMC and the PMC retain identities as truly international denominations? Or would a divorce, over what is primarily a debate within the United States, include a decision that liberates United Methodists in Europe, Asia, Africa, and Latin America from institutional ties to American Methodism? In the Philippines Central Conference, there are twenty-six annual conferences. They are currently grouped into three Episcopal Areas. Might some of these conferences choose the OMC and others choose the PMC? Or would this be the time when Methodist institutions in the Philippines are set free to become autonomous and to have an ecclesial independence like the political independence their country has enjoyed since 1946?

34 The conference in New York took thirty-five days; it was the longest General Conference in Methodism.

not involve as many complex considerations as would have to be managed today.

- *First*, the Methodists who sought to separate in the middle of the nineteenth century were basically in an institution within one nation, the United States of America.

- *Second*, the two church bodies that emerged from the divorce were, for the most part, geographically and politically identifiable. Slavery was the divisive issue. The Methodist Episcopal Church, South, situated itself where slavery was legal. And the Methodist Episcopal Church found its home where slavery was illegal.

- *Third*, there were no organizational units between the annual conferences and the General Conference, such as jurisdictional or central conferences, to be managed.

- *Fourth*, in 1844 the only voting delegates at the General Conference were clergy, because laity had not yet been granted the right to vote at the General Conference or annual conference levels. And they were all men, because women were not yet allowed to be ordained.

- *Fifth*, Methodism in 1844 understood itself as "connectional" rather than as a collection of congregations and clergy. The connection endured a divorce in 1844; in 2019, a divorce would have to accommodate thousands of pieces of a puzzle.

- *Sixth*, the impact of such a divorce on the "local church" was not seriously at issue in 1844, because Methodism did not even use the phrase "local church" in its official jargon until the twentieth century.

- *Seventh*, the denomination did not have the bureaucracy of commissions, boards, agencies, councils, or a "table" that The United Methodist Church has built.

- *Eighth*, every bureaucratic body that is incorporated with assets and obligations in the current church will have to be accommodated in the "divorce" agreement.

- *Ninth*, institutions owned by some entity in the church (for example, American University, which is owned by the General Board of Higher Education and Ministry of The United Methodist Church, and Emory

University, which is owned by the Southeastern Jurisdictional Conference) might go to civil court to seek relief from the terms of the "divorce" agreement. Vanderbilt University went to civil court in Tennessee and prevailed over the church in the late nineteenth and early twentieth centuries.

• *Tenth*, the Judicial Council did not exist in 1844. When delegates developed the terms of the "divorce" during the General Conference in 1844, they only needed affirmation by the bishops. In 2019, if the General Conference adopts a divorce agreement, 20 percent of the delegates may vote to appeal to the Judicial Council. And 20 percent of the delegates at a central or jurisdictional conference could appeal it.[35]

So United Methodists, based on their disagreements over homosexuality, might decide to go through a divorce and be rid of their ecclesiastical adversaries. The model of divorce is available through a historic precedent.

However, in the twenty-first century, these proceedings will be extremely messy. Nobody can predict whether all of the entities linked to The United Methodist Church would settle for the terms of the divorce that might be negotiated. Nobody can be sure how much civil court activity might follow the church's decision to divide, how long such litigation could take, or how much it would cost. Nobody can be sure how many members would choose simply to walk away from their local churches and their financial pledges, rather than be ensnarled in disputes that could be as difficult after a division as they are before it.

Of course, a schism along the lines of this scheme would also mean the end of a body known as The United Methodist Church. The institution by that name is respected, but it is hardly viewed as venerable. It was formed in 1968 by merger of The Methodist Church and the Evangelical United Brethren. So The United Methodist Church will mark fifty years of existence while the denomination is deciding whether it will survive. After two millennia of Christianity, fifty years is barely a dot on a timeline. That dot, however, is not insignificant.

The merger in 1968 ended racial segregation as a primary organizing

---

35 *The Book of Discipline of The United Methodist Church 2012*, ¶¶ 2609.1 and 2609.3, pp. 768–69.

principle of mainstream Methodism. The jurisdictional system that was devised in 1939 had imposed a racist, iniquitous, inequitable entity known as the "Central Jurisdiction" on the reunited church. It had replaced a regional division (North/South) with a racial one (black/white). The 1968 merger retained the system of jurisdictions, but their boundaries were drawn by geography not by race. So the creation of United Methodism ended official, institutionalized segregation.

Additionally, in its fifty years, The United Methodist Church made other progress. It welcomed women into leadership positions that were previously occupied only by men, including the office of bishop. It developed programs that promoted equity and justice in ethnic and racial diversity. It became more global, with a radical change in proportion of members from nations other than the United States.[36] It took an active role in transitions in Central and Eastern Europe after the demise of the Soviet Union, including the creation of a theological school in Russia. It dared to draft social principles on matters affecting the entire world, like immigration and climate change. It engaged ecumenical and interfaith partners across national and ecclesial boundaries in forming new dialogues that fostered a spirit of reconciliation.

And, in its fifty years, The United Methodist Church chose to be a leader among all Methodists on matters of shared interest. The denomination led in scholarship, with a commitment to publish a definitive academic edition of *The Works of John Wesley.* The denomination emerged as the major financial supporter of the World Methodist Council and the World Methodist Conference. The denomination contributed individual voices of leadership in society and in the world, including—but not limited to—bishops of The United Methodist Church. Episcopal leaders such as Woodie White, Minerva Carcaño, and David Lawson showed the people entrusted to their care that effective ministry has secular and sacred dimensions and that it involves global as well as local disciplinary duties. Such vision is an intangible asset, but whether it could be conveyed to both divorcing church parties is unknown. How it might be built into a schismatic agreement is baffling.

If there were to be a divorce in The United Methodist Church, even those

36 According to the most recent data available, about 42 percent of United Methodists today live in a country other than the United States.

who are sure it is necessary and wise will have to acknowledge that it will be messy. It will also be sad. It could cost a lot. And a lot could be lost if the denomination disappears in death.

DISCONNECT

Divorce is not the only option. And the death of The United Methodist Church is not an inevitable outcome. The church as an institution could survive the current crisis and still let its internal antagonists find a way to be rid of each other. But instead of a divorce, the disgruntled might just be allowed to disconnect. We have experience with disconnecting.

Methodists received the nickname by which they are known because the founder received criticism for devising *methods* to practice Christian discipleship. John Wesley accepted the epithet as an asset. He adopted "Methodist" as the name for his movement.

And, to a remarkable extent, denominations that bear the name Methodist have continued to use *methods* for almost everything. Within the Constitution and the *Discipline* of The United Methodist Church, there are methods for entities to disconnect from it. Those methods can be used to grant local churches liberty from the denomination, to give institutions founded by the church an opportunity to function without church dominance, and even to protect the assets of a conference or congregation. At least two annual conferences in recent years used such methods to accommodate local churches seeking separation from the denomination.

One of the prominent ministries on which Methodists focus has been education. John Wesley founded Kingswood School in Bath, England, in the early days of the Methodist movement.[37] Francis Asbury and Thomas Coke founded Cokesbury College in the earliest days of organizing a Methodist Church in North America.[38] Only the Roman Catholic Church—a much

---

37 Wesley established the school in 1748. Its motto is indicative of an intense Methodist commitment to education and the consistency of Methodists' convictions that their endeavors in mission were intended to achieve great goals. The motto of Kingswood is *In Via Recta Celeriter* ("In The Right Way Quickly").

38 Cokesbury College was conceived during the Christmas Conference in 1784, which American Methodists consider the start of the Methodist Episcopal Church in the United States of America. It opened in 1787. However, John Wesley was outraged that Coke and Asbury called their institution a "college" rather than a school, and he was furious that they named it for themselves.

larger Christian institution—has built schools, colleges, and universities in numbers comparable to those that the Methodists created.

The methods varied. Catholics typically founded their educational institutions by the church *per se* or by religious orders. Methodists founded schools and colleges either through the church or through individuals of faith.

Some, for example Duke University, were established by Methodist persons and organizations but were not actually owned or controlled by the church. Yet they retained a Methodist form in certain ways, such as the pattern of the principal worship experiences on campus. And they retained a Methodist influence with specified seats on their boards of trustees reserved for the church.

Some, notably Southern Methodist University and Emory University, arose from collaborations between the church and their respective communities in their states. Both, however, were established as church-owned institutions and have technically remained under church ownership.

Some, like Boston University and Drew University, began as theological schools for preparing church leaders and expanded into broader fields of study in the process of becoming universities. Their theological schools retained relationships with the church, while the rest of each university operated independently from the church.

Some, such as Wesleyan University, Syracuse University, and the University of Southern California, were started as universities. They were closely affiliated with the church or were under denominational control. Later, they became independent of the church.

Some colleges were established in the era of racial segregation to meet the education needs of African American students, who were otherwise excluded from most opportunities for higher education. Such Methodist schools include Dillard in Louisiana, Wiley in Texas, Bethune-Cookman in Florida, Wilberforce in Ohio, Clark Atlanta in Georgia, and Claflin in South Carolina.

Some regional colleges were founded by annual conferences and have varying degrees of connection to the church today. Among them are Baker in Kansas, Centenary in Louisiana, Hendrix in Arkansas, LaGrange in Georgia, Lycoming in Pennsylvania, Millsaps in Mississippi, and Simpson in Iowa.

And some college preparatory schools were founded. Only a few of them remain in operation with any links to the church. Two examples are Lydia Patterson Institute in Texas, which still is strongly tied to the church, and

Wyoming Seminary in Pennsylvania, which only maintains modest denominational relationships.

Many of these Methodist connections with education go unnoticed nowadays. The church provides a relatively small—and in many cases, an extremely tiny—portion of the institutions' budgets. In addition, the percentage of the students and faculty who have a Methodist affiliation never was a major point of emphasis for most of these schools, and it remains rather small. The reason is that the church saw itself as committed to education for missional purposes—to reform the continent—but not as a means to grow the church.

In time, disconnecting the church from its educational institutions came naturally and occurred by mutual agreement. Some were possibly initiated by a desire of the university to be free from church control. Sometimes, the church simply recognized that institutions of higher learning were more accountable to regulatory bodies than met church interests.

There were occasions, though, when a revolution not an evolution caused change. Some of the separations were far from amicable. Vanderbilt University's freedom from church control involved adversarial battles between bishops of the Methodist Episcopal Church, South, and the board of trustees of the university. Eventually, the state courts of Tennessee ruled in favor of the Vanderbilt trustees.

Methodists founded other institutional ministries besides education as a part of the movement's mission. Some of those institutions became independent of the church too. And such separations happened not because the denomination was stepping away from public or societal ministries. It was a way of protecting church assets.

One of the most prominent public ministries for American Methodists has been in the area of health care. Across the nation one can still hear the word *Methodist* in names of hospitals. But the church's commitment to health care was even broader. Methodists built homes to provide care for children. Initially, such facilities were intended to meet the needs of orphans, whose parents died or did not exhibit any capacity to care for their offspring. When "orphanages" acquired a social stigma or developed a reduced profile in the safety net of services for needy children, some of the institutions moved into different program directions. For example, The United Methodist Children's Home in New York became a multisite, multipurpose residential and outpatient treatment center for addicted or troubled youth.

Methodists also built homes for aging persons. Initially, many were communal residences that provided housing and health care for retired clergy, deaconesses, or others whose resources were too limited for independent living. But extensive campuses having private villas, apartment buildings with assisted living, and centers for acute care also became part of comprehensive approaches to health care in church-related facilities.

Many forces drove such institutions to disconnect from the church. Most dramatic among them was a case involving the Pacific Homes Corporation in 1978. It was an event that led many church-related institutions for health care to separate from the church. And it also led to the disclaimer that has appeared in *The Book of Discipline* since 1984 that The United Methodist Church, *per se*, does not actually exist as an entity.

To summarize this complex matter very briefly, the Pacific Homes Corporation was a United Methodist mission to provide housing for aging persons. Through its "life contracts," Pacific Homes accepted lump sum payments from residents and guaranteed them housing for the rest of their lives. However, in time, it became clear that the amount of money committed in life contracts by these residents was insufficient to cover the costs of housing them for their increasingly longer lives. The Pacific Homes Corporation filed for bankruptcy in 1977. Then numerous residents filed suit against the corporation—and the church—demanding that the life contracts be honored. When the case was settled, the connections between the church and its health-care institutions had changed permanently.

One outcome of the case was the determination that The United Methodist Church as a whole is not an entity that can be sued. A grievance against Pacific Homes could not pursue a liability claim against the rest of the denomination. The institutions and all of the local churches in United Methodism are secure from such legal action. In short, The United Methodist Church is not an entity. It does not exist in law.[39]

Another outcome of the case was a decision to disconnect the church from health-care institutions that it had built, operated, or controlled. Steps were taken to make them legally separate from any church agencies or conferences that owned them. Most of them disconnected from the church by establishing independent corporations.

In effect, the church came to view the health-care institutions not as

---

39   See the aforementioned ¶ 141 of *The Book of Discipline of The United Methodist Church 2016*.

endeavors for mission but primarily as assets or (potential) liabilities. In many cases, the church simply gave them away rather than attempt to sell them or close them and liquidate the assets. It was a device to disconnect what had once been perceived as an important ministry of the church and release it to the private sector of society.

Something similar could happen if the church and other institutions it owns and/or controls were to choose to disconnect. This time, it could occur as part of a process that arises from a denominational division over homosexuality. The United Methodist Church (through its constituent conferences, corporations, or agencies) could disconnect itself from many of its assets. It could choose to give away—if not liquidate—its institutions in health care, housing, education, or other endeavors.

What about a local church? Could a congregation disconnect itself from its annual conference and denomination? Could an annual conference liquidate a local church? The short answer to each question is no, but the answers have to be qualified.

If a local church desires to disconnect from the denomination, the methods to do so are available. And those methods are specified in and required by church law. These methods would enable a local church to retain control over its assets—its property, in particular—and continue to function as a congregation without the constraints of being connected to The United Methodist Church. Two basic methods exist for local churches to achieve independence by taking actions under church law to disconnect from the denomination.

First, a local church could change its denominational affiliation by leaving The United Methodist Church as one part of a process that involves its affiliating with another denomination. According to the provisions in ¶ 2548.2 of the *Discipline*, there are two ways to do this. A congregation could take steps to become affiliated with a body that, along with The United Methodist Church, is one of the Pan-Methodist denominations.[40] Or a congregation could take steps to affiliate with "another evangelical denomination."[41]

---

40   The member churches in the Pan-Methodist Commission are the African Methodist Episcopal Church, the African Methodist Episcopal Zion Church, the African Union Methodist Protestant Church, the Christian Methodist Episcopal Church, the Union American Methodist Episcopal Church, and The United Methodist Church. See ¶ 433.2, p. 355 of *The Book of Discipline of The United Methodist Church 2016*.

41   The 2016 Discipline does not specify the meaning of "evangelical denomination" in ¶ 2548.2, p. 770 or provide a list of qualifying denominations.

There are three required steps to disconnect by this method.

1. During an official meeting at the local church level,[42] a "request" to change the denominational affiliation would have to be adopted.

2. The following three parties would have to grant "consent" to this request:

   • the bishop who presides over the annual conference where the local church is affiliated;

   • a majority of the district superintendents in that annual conference; and

   • the district board of church location and building in the district where the local church is situated.

3. Based on the "request" that has been adopted and the "consent" that has already been obtained, the annual conference then "may instruct and direct the board of trustees of a local church to deed the property" to one of the Pan-Methodist denominations or to an "evangelical denomination" as provided in ¶ 2548.2 of the 2016 *Discipline*.

Action by a local church alone is not sufficient to achieve separation. The other steps are also necessary. The "consent" must be granted by all three entities beyond the local church, and any one of the three would effectively be able to "veto" the effort by a congregation to disconnect. Also, the annual conference is at liberty not to concur with the "request" from the local church even if the other three parties granted their "consent" to the request. But the steps are clear, and the process is clean. With this method, a local church could be released from its affiliation with The United Methodist Church and could retain use of its accustomed property.

Yet ownership of the property would not be transferred to the local church that had asked to disconnect from The United Methodist Church. Instead, the ownership of the property would be moved to the authority of "another evangelical denomination" or the authority of one of the Pan-Methodist denominations. Therefore, this method would not be suitable

42 The meeting would have to be a "charge conference" (see ¶¶ 246–47, pp. 173–78, of the *Discipline*), a "church conference" (see ¶ 248, pp. 178–79, of the *Discipline*), or—since local church property would be involved—possibly a "church local conference" (see ¶ 2527, pp. 750–51, of the *Discipline*).

in a situation where a local church wished simply to become an independent, unaffiliated, freestanding congregation. Moreover, this method would only affect the local church property. The members would have to be transferred to, or be embraced by, the denomination to which the deed for the property was moved. Of course, some sort of "comity agreement"[43] could cover that detail regarding membership.

And none of this would directly affect the appointed clergy who had been serving a local church that sought to "disconnect" from The United Methodist Church. The clergy would have other options: to request an appointment elsewhere in the annual conference of The United Methodist Church; to seek transfer to the denomination that will receive the property, perhaps in the hope of being assigned, appointed, or called into the ministry of that local church; or to withdraw from the ordained ministry in The United Methodist Church and hope for some other vocational opportunity elsewhere in the near future.

Second, a local church could initiate action to disconnect from the denomination entirely, and it could become an independent entity. But initiating the process is not a guarantee that its outcome will meet all of the expectations of the local church, that it would make financial sense, or that it will result in happiness for all concerned.

Nevertheless, the steps are quite clear. They build on a premise that The United Methodist Church is a connectional body—not a collection of local churches and clergy, but an organic "connection" of all the elements that together constitute the denomination. It entails layers of conferences, incorporated and unincorporated institutions, orders and offices of clergy, committees, councils, agencies, boards, and other connectional entities. A local church could approach a district superintendent and request, under the terms of the 2016 *Discipline* in ¶ 2549, that the church be "closed" because it "no longer serves the purpose for which it was organized" or it "is no longer used, kept, or maintained by its membership as a place of divine worship of The United Methodist Church."[44] To get the result it desires, a disconnecting congregation would need cooperation from district superintendents,

---

43   The phrase *comity agreement* appears in ¶ 2548.2, p. 770, of the *Discipline*.

44   Other provisions in the *Discipline* would have to be honored, including ¶¶ 201–4 and 2529.1
(b)3, pp. 147–48 and 753.

the district board of church location and building, conference trustees, the bishop, and the annual conference. But it could disconnect from the connection. As a "closed" church, the property by prearrangement could then be sold by the trustees of the annual conference to a corporation that may consist of some former members of the "closed" church. The "connection" would remain intact, while the congregation that sought to separate from the denomination would have its freedom.

Other denominations describe their structures as a "connectional church" system. But none of them has the same interrelated intricacy of design or function. Presbyterians describe their polity as "connectional," but their congregations have substantially more autonomy than local churches in United Methodism. Religious groups with hierarchical systems, like the Roman Catholic Church or the Church of Jesus Christ of Latter Day Saints, are connected vertically but not in multidimensional ways as United Methodists are.

The difference is clear whenever someone from another church tradition becomes (or seeks to become) a United Methodist. Clergy seeking to transfer and to be accepted as ordained ministers by The United Methodist Church may ask about the address of the "national office" or the person at the "denominational headquarters" to whom they should write.[45] Laity who are familiar with a "congregational" perspective ask why they cannot vote on their church's public policies regarding issues in society rather than letting a denomination's Social Principles speak for them. Clergy and laity both wonder why they cannot choose their own places of service or pastoral leaders.[46]

But it is most apparent when considering matters of church property. Since 1763, when John Wesley drafted a "Model Deed" for managing the chapels and other pieces of real estate used by his Methodist movement, the laws of the Methodist church tradition have understood property as a "connectional" asset. Wesley's eighteenth-century "Model Deed" became a "trust clause" in the *Discipline* of the church. In its current formulation, that clause is written this way:

---

45   In The United Methodist Church, there is no such thing as a national office or headquarters. See ¶ 141, p. 102.

46   Ministry in United Methodism is based on a principle of being sent to a place of mission, not called by a congregation.

> All properties of United Methodist local churches and other United Methodist agencies and institutions are held, *in trust*, for the benefit of the entire denomination, and ownership and usage of church of church property is subject to the *Discipline*. This trust requirement is an essential element of the historic polity of The United Methodist Church or its predecessor denominations or communions and has been part of the *Discipline* since 1797. It reflects the connectional structure of the Church by ensuring that the property will be used solely for purposes consonant with the mission of the entire denomination as set forth in the *Discipline*. The trust requirement is thus a fundamental expression of United Methodism, whereby local churches and other agencies and institutions within the denomination are both held accountable to and benefit from their connection with the entire worldwide Church.[47]

The law of the church is adamant about this principle, calling it "irrevocable."[48] And, although the law of the church specifies that the "trust clause" is to be included in deeds or other documents associated with the ownership and use of church property, "the absence of a trust clause . . . in deeds and conveyances executed previously or in the future shall in no way exclude a local church or church agency, or the board of trustees of either, of its responsibility and accountability to The United Methodist Church. . . ."[49]

Decisions by the Judicial Council of The United Methodist Church have made it clear that the "trust clause" covers institutions that are owned by the church. It does not apply solely or only to local church properties.[50] But it certainly does apply to properties that congregations have owned, maintained, improved, and financed.

So any local church that seeks to disconnect from the denomination must address the mandate of the "trust clause." And any such endeavor must comply with the terms of church law in order to achieve separation from the church.[51]

The first step in such an effort would happen in the governing body of a local church, which is described in the distinctively Methodist manner. The

---

47   *The Book of Discipline of The United Methodist Church 2016*, ⁋ 2501.1, p. 733.

48   See ⁋ 2501.2, p. 733 of the 2016 *Discipline*.

49   See ⁋ 2503.6, pp. 735–36 of the 2016 *Discipline*.

50   See Judicial Council Decisions 166, 874, and 1113.

51   See ⁋ 2529.1b(3), p. 753 of the 2016 *Discipline*.

local governing body is a kind of conference—either a "charge conference" or a "church conference" or a "church local" conference.

It should be noted that there are less dire ways to disconnect than dividing from the denomination. There are operational as well as organizational ways to "disconnect." And some units within United Methodism already have. For example, the only body with responsibility for the character and qualifications of ordained ministers is the annual conference. The United Methodist "connection" has adopted church laws that stipulate educational requirements that a candidate for ordination must meet, the theological issues that a candidate for ordination must address, and the educational institutions where one may receive a theological degree in order to satisfy the criteria of church law. But the annual conference is the only body that can determine if the standards specified by the criteria have been met. Operationally, the clergy in an annual conference—through its board of ordained ministry—could find various ways that are consistent with church law to approve only candidates for ordained ministry who earned theological degrees at just a few (or one or two) of the denominationally approved theological schools.

As the 2016 General Conference approached, there were petitions that sought to codify this operational practice in church law. The petitions wanted annual conferences to have the authority to decide which theological schools were satisfactory for theological education of their candidates for ordained ministry. While the General Conference did not adopt the language of these petitions, some United Methodists made it very clear that they wanted to disconnect operationally from the denomination on matters of theological education for their future pastors.

Within the current climate of The United Methodist Church, where significant amounts of energy are being directed toward the possibility of schism, there are methods to disconnect from the church. Congregations, corporations, and clergy have pathways in the *Discipline* for doing so. Local churches, colleges, hospitals, and others could find a way to disconnect and retain use of their properties. Some of these devices are already euphemistically described as ways to "loosen" the connection.

None of them could achieve schism independently, arbitrarily, or by acting alone. But political pressures might encourage accommodations to the interests of those who desire to divide United Methodism by disconnecting from United Methodism. That could still mean The United Methodist Church would exist. It might have tens of thousands of local churches, tens of thousands of clergy, unknown amounts of financial assets, and an equally unknown amount of financial obligations. But that might not matter, unless it believes it has a mission that is as big as the world.

QUESTIONS FOR DISCUSSION

1. How would you describe the prospects for division, schism, or separation in the church?

   - Very unlikely?

   - Possible?

   - Probable?

   - Almost certain?

2. What are the most divisive forces in the church today?

   - Disputes over homosexuality, abortion, or other matters of public debate?

   - Matters of Christian doctrine and church law?

   - Internal church matters, such as money or property or administrative control?

   - Loss of connection with some demographic groups identifiable by age or race?

3. Was it appropriate for denominations to divide over slavery in the nineteenth century?

4. Which is more painful with regard to divorce?

   - Going through the process of separation and division to end the relationship?

   - Staying together, even in a relationship that seems very problematic?

5. Which would be the best outcome for the denomination?

   - Remain as we are, even if that means a permanent condition of distress?

   - Divide into parts or pieces, even if that means a very costly process?

   - Find a way to unify in a common mission, even if that means adjusting our views?

PART FOUR

DELIVERANCE

Deliver me, O Lord,
From death eternal on that fearful day,
When the heavens and the earth shall be moved,
When thou shalt come to judge the world by fire.

Libera Me (*Deliver Me*) from *Requiem*

DECISIONS

In a meeting with bishops, board members, and executives of the denomination, a United Methodist layperson who is a business consultant from Texas reported on the state of the church. He said that United Methodism is in crisis and has to act. Specifically, he "warned that the church needed to quickly adopt a credible and metrics driven plan to arrest the plunge in worship attendance. If it failed to do so, he projected that by 2030 the denomination would slide into permanent decline and face collapse by 2050."[1]

In a meeting near a tree, according to the first lines of a play by a Nobel Prize–winning author, two friends find themselves immobilized by their circumstances. They discuss matters of faith, death, and life. They conclude that they are incapable of making any response to their crisis. They are prisoners of inaction, locked into a hapless and hopeless fate, while imagining that a liberator named Godot will deliver them without requiring any cooperation on their part.

> estragon: Nothing to be done.
> vladimir: I'm beginning to come round to that opinion . . .[2]

In a meeting near a crossroads named Haran, a man known as Abram received a revelation from God. There was no crisis in his life. But God offered him a new identity, summoning him to a mission and saying, according to Genesis, "Go from your country and your kindred and your father's house to the land that I will show you. . . . Abram went."[3]

MISSION

The saga of Abraham is one of the foundational stories for the people of God. It begins in the opening verses of Genesis 12 as a revelation from the Lord to a man who was then called Abram. He, his wife Sarai, his nephew Lot, and their extended family lived in a place named Haran. Abram's father,

---

1   Walter Fenton, "Plunge in Worship Attendance," *Good News Magazine*, January 24, 2017.

2   Samuel Beckett, *Waiting for Godot: A Tragicomedy in Two Acts* (New York: Grove Press, 1954) 7.

3   Genesis 12:1, 4.

who had taken the clan to dwell there, had died there. The family expected to stay and enjoy a satisfying life.

Then came the revelation from the Lord, inviting Abram to leave. It arrived as a bundle of immensely mysterious promises but with no practical guidance or timetable for their fulfillment. Abram was simply summoned to leave the circumstances into which he had settled and go to an unknown, unnamed place. Beyond that minimal information, God promised to reveal everything at some unspecified time. In any case, Abram went.

The invitation from the Lord was the epitome of uncertainty. Abram's response was exemplary. For his act of faith, he has been honored throughout the ages. Muslims, Christians, and Jews are his heirs. The apostle Paul wrote to the Romans that Abram was "the father of all of us" who "share the faith" in which he believed.[4] The letter to the Hebrews praises the "faith" by which "he set out, not knowing where he was going."[5]

As Abram's story unfolds in Genesis, he faces immense challenges. He has to alter his understanding of the definition of family. He has to accept a change in identity and take a new name, *Abraham*.[6] At one point, he was declared "as good as dead."[7] At the end of his time on earth, he "died in faith without having received the promises."[8]

Yet his faithful journey did not really end in death. Instead, the Bible says, he is waiting for others who will come from east and west to share in the heavenly feast, and he is waiting in the realm of heaven to greet the dead either with the embrace of his bosom or with words of judgment.[9] Meanwhile, on earth, his legacy endures. His story is a matter of death and life.

Everything in the biblical saga of Abraham is framed by the mission on which God sent him, the identity that this mission gave him, the boundless promises that God embedded in the mission, and the choices Abraham felt empowered to make because he trusted God's promises. Others who feel perplexed by their problems or confronted by their crises might say,

---

4   Romans 4:16–17.

5   Hebrews 11:8.

6   Genesis 17:5.

7   Romans 4:19; Hebrews 11:12.

8   Hebrews 11:13.

9   Matthew 8:11; Luke 16:22.

"We must do something to make a difference" or "We cannot do anything that will make a difference." But Abraham allowed his life to be defined by what he was invited to trust. He embraced the mission, relied on the promises, accepted the Lord's invitation, and treasured whatever might lie ahead through God's gift.

If Abraham's mission of faithfulness was devout, it had plenty of imperfections. His missteps and mistakes are too many to recount. But, as the apostle Paul wrote and as the ages have echoed, it was Abraham's faith not his actions that formed the basis of his relationship with God. "No distrust made him waver concerning the promise of God."[10]

People of faith do not define the mission on which we are sent. It defines us. We discover what the mission requires of us through responding in faith as it calls. Trusting the promises of God becomes our mission. We discern as a community what "has seemed good to the Holy Spirit and to us."[11] We act, but not by our own instincts. We hope, but not on the basis of our own strength. We believe, despite evident reasons to despair.

Our mission defines who we are. It delivers us from whoever we were. And it directs us to whatever we will be. But it may not be easy to describe, explain, express, or state what the mission is. Crafting a concise statement of mission may be as difficult as answering a psychological question of one's personal identity ("Who am I?") or a spiritual question of the church's identity ("Who are we?").

Methodists have expressed our mission in a number of ways. John Wesley's formula for stating the mission of the Methodists stressed "the reform of the nation and more particularly the church . . . spreading scriptural holiness."[12] In his view this meant both personal discipline and social holiness, both private piety and public pressure to embrace all the promises of God. In a single frame, he focused both on personal salvation and public welfare. He saw spiritual significance in addressing both the sin that imprisons souls and the souls that are sequestered in prisons.

---

10 Romans 4:20.

11 Acts 15:28.

12 W. R. Ward, "Was There a Methodist Evangelistic Strategy in the Eighteenth Century?" in *England's Long Reformation: 1500–1800*, ed. Nicholas Tyacke (London: UCL Press, 1998), 290. See also *The 'Large' Minutes* in *The Works of John Wesley: The Methodist Societies and Minutes of the Conference*, vol. 10, ed. Rack, 845.

The Methodists who met in Baltimore at a Christmas Conference in 1784 wrote a mission statement that differed only slightly from Wesley's. They said their purpose was "to reform the continent and to spread scriptural holiness over these lands."[13] They too sought to deliver individuals from their demons and to deliver society from its sufferings.

During subsequent decades, descriptions of the Methodists' mission became less concise and less clear. Then, a bit more than two centuries after the Christmas Conference, The United Methodist Church at its 1996 General Conference put a mission statement into two sentences and placed it in a preamble to the chapter of *The Book of Discipline* on the local church.

> The mission of the Church is to make disciples of Jesus Christ.
> Local churches provide the most significant arena through which
> disciple-making occurs.[14]

Four years later, the 2000 General Conference kept the same mission statement but relocated it from the narrow terms of "local church" to the broader heading of "The Mission and Ministry of the Church." Also, instead of burying it in a preamble, *The Book of Discipline* assigned it to a designated paragraph number. So it was easier to find.

Eight years later, in 2008, the General Conference revised the opening sentence of the mission statement and added a phrase to state the purpose of disciple making.

> ¶ 120. *The Mission*—The mission of the Church is to make disciples
> of Jesus Christ *for the transformation of the world.* Local churches
> provide the most significant arena through which disciple-making
> occurs.[15]

In 2016, the General Conference added still another phrase to the statement.

> ¶ 120. *The Mission*—The mission of the Church is to make dis-
> ciples of Jesus Christ for the transformation of the world. Local

---

13 Ward, "Was There a Methodist Evangelistic Strategy," 292. See also Richey, "United Methodist Doctrine and Teaching on the Nature, Mission and Faithfulness of the Church," p. 18.

14 *The Book of Discipline of The United Methodist Church 1996*, 114.

15 *The Book of Discipline of the United Methodist Church 2008*, ¶ 120, p. 87; and 2012, ¶ 120, p. 91 (emphasis added).

churches *and extension ministries of the Church* provide the most significant arena through which disciple-making occurs.[16]

These recent amendments may seem to be relatively minor changes. As a train of editorial revisions, adding a phrase or changing a location in the *Discipline*, the words do not change the substance of the mission statement. But there are significant differences between this mission statement and those crafted by John Wesley and by the institutional founders of American Methodism.

First, the current statement focuses United Methodism's mission on the formation of *individuals* into disciples. It sees individuals as exclusive agents of mission and as the instruments for the transformation of the world while practicing discipleship. The mission of the church is aimed only at individuals, not at the systems that hold people captive, and it calls individuals—not the connection—to be the agency for transforming the world.

Second, the current mission statement focuses on the *localized* ministry settings (local congregations and "extension ministries") that make individual disciples. There is no role for the Methodist connection as a whole. Local ministries—not regional or global or connectional ministries—are the main mechanisms for discipleship and transformation. To the extent that the church addresses the crises of the age—substance abuse, domestic violence, global peace, access to health care, refugee resettlement, climate change, and immigration, for example—localized ministries are the sole means for delivering God's creatures and God's creation from the scourges that afflict them.

In effect, the current form of the mission statement serves as another example of what Russell Richey referred to as "ensmalling"[17] the church. It reduces the institutional profile of United Methodism to a collection of discrete localized entities and to the footprints of individual disciples. It narrows responsibility for Christian mission to separated centers and segments of history. It sees God's promises focused in the small dimensions of individuals' times and spaces. It even allows congregations to limit their mission and

---

16   *The Book of Discipline of the United Methodist Church 2016*, ¶ 120, p. 93 (emphasis added).

17   Richey, *The Methodist Conference in America*, 180f.

vision to local considerations and to avoid any encounters with the crises of the day if that is the local church's preference.[18]

Unlike a 1779 conference in Fluvanna County, Virginia, at which Methodists as a community inveighed against slavery as an institution,[19] a statement of Christian mission that imagines the church as a collection of individual disciples can authorize us to shrink from addressing sinful structures. It lacks a sense of the church as a faithful system that publicly confronts the world's demonic systems. It misconstrues the forces faced by the church and misrepresents the fears we need to relieve. And, furthermore, it minimizes our clout as a connection in the public arena.

Francis Asbury understood the importance of a mobilized ecclesial system in a mission to reform the continent and spread scriptural holiness. He "got the American preachers off their bottoms," wrote W. R. Ward.[20] Today, most of the church's leaders have hit the wall that limits an "ensmalled" church, and many wonder how the body of Christ can be mobilized again to reform the continent and spread scriptural holiness.

A United Methodist bishop, serving an Episcopal Area within one of the southern states along the border between the United States and Mexico, told about a day when two bishops visited the governor of their state. They asked him to adopt immigration policies that are consistent with the Social Principles of The United Methodist Church.[21] But the governor replied that he saw only two persons sitting in his office. He told them to come back when they might have twenty thousand people supporting the church's position on immigration. Those two bishops knew that there are far, far more than twenty thousand United Methodists in the state. But they did not feel free to claim that they had the clout of a whole church in support of their plea. They were just two individual believers.

It is worth asking whether the current formulation of the denomination's mission limits or "ensmalls" the church in the twenty-first century. It is worth asking whether the mission statement in today's *Discipline* is sufficiently

---

18 To borrow a phrase from Scripture, this is what happens when the community of faith devolves into a collection of individuals who do what is right in their own eyes (Judges 17:6, 21:25; Proverbs 21:2).

19 Richey, *The Methodist Conference in America*, 28.

20 W. R. Ward, "Was There a Methodist Evangelistic Strategy," 296.

21 See *The Book of Discipline of The United Methodist Church 2016*, ¶ 162 H, pp. 122–123.

Abrahamic in its faith in God's promises for a future community. It is worth asking whether the denomination's current statement of mission adequately describes the capabilities of Methodism in the world. It is worth asking whether global Methodism, having shrunk in its self-understanding into a smaller identity of limited mission, has decided to sit still and to wait until it dies.

There is little doubt that United Methodism casts a smaller shadow in America than it did decades ago. At the time of the reunion of three Methodist churches in 1939, what was newly named as "The Methodist Church" claimed to have "a membership of approximately 8,000,000"[22] in the United States. At that time, the nation had about 132 million people, so 6 percent of them were Methodists. By 2016, the population of the country had increased to 326 million, while the number of United Methodists in the nation dropped to 7 million. So, nowadays, only 2 percent of Americans are United Methodists.

Since The Methodist Church and Evangelical United Brethren merged in 1968, the denomination has closed or lost nearly one-fourth of its local churches. In its numbers of members and congregations, United Methodism is shrinking. But those numbers can be misleading. Any analysis of United Methodism in the United States today has to consider the context of Americans' attitudes toward religion.

In 1992, only 6 percent of Americans rejected religious affiliation.[23] Today, that is closer to 25 percent for the whole country. It is even higher for the millennial generation. In addition, there is a sociocultural dimension to these data. Church attendance in the United States has declined twice as much among whites without a college education as among whites with a college degree.[24] United Methodism shares those trends.

One analysis of the data has shown that membership has increased in the ethnic minority constituencies in The United Methodist Church. It has only been among white members that a decline has actually occurred.[25]

Another data analytic says that the average age of United Methodists

---

22   *Doctrines and Disciplines of The Methodist Church, 1939,* eds. John W. Langdale, Alfred F. Smith, T. Leroy Hooper (New York: The Methodist Book Concern, 1939), 7.

23   Peter Beinart, "Breaking Faith," *Atlantic,* April 2017.

24   This is from a study by W. Bradford Wilcox, cited by Peter Beinart in "Breaking Faith."

25   David W. Scott, *UM & GLOBAL,* March 9, 2017.

is in the low sixties. That makes it an older demographic, to be sure. But it is the age cohort that ranks at the crest of most persons' careers, as well as their wisdom and their earning capacity. And it is the group with the deepest, richest pool of experience. Besides, it is the average age for cohorts other than United Methodists. It is similar to the average age of viewers for many of the news media powerhouses in the United States. The average FOX News audience member is sixty-six years of age. The viewers of MSNBC average sixty-three years of age. And the viewers of CNN have an average age of sixty-one years.[26] New forms of social media clearly have replaced networks' monopolies in certain age groups. But the networks' audiences are still measured in the tens of millions. So they can scarcely be dismissed. They deliver information about which others tweet.

Likewise, millions of people attend United Methodist worship each week, so they cannot be ignored. United Methodists can constitute a formidable presence. They remain an important public constituency, even if their numerical imprint is not proportionally the same as it once was.

Yet it is still a sizable imprint. There are more United Methodist congregations in the United States than there are post offices. There is a United Methodist church presence in roughly 90 percent of the counties in the country. Eight percent of the members of Congress are United Methodists. The church appears to be growing in racial diversity.

There is more. Methodism holds a significant place in the popular imagination. Its image has been noted in novels and referenced on screens. Its candor about sin has given Methodism a solid profile. Its commitment to social justice is a symbol of prophecy. And its reputation for doing good works has even made it the object of parody. Consider these:

- In a 2004 network television drama about a dysfunctional family, a woman prepares for her grandchild's baptism. She objects to a text in the United Methodist ritual that the pastor plans to use. The grandmother finds all the references to deliverance from "the spiritual forces of wickedness ... evil powers of this world, and ... sin" to be unwelcome. She tells the pastor she deems what Methodism says about sinfulness

---

26   John Koblin, *New York Times*, December 29, 2016, B-2.

to be odd. "I thought that you Methodists were a more moderate sort," she says.[27]

- In one of John Grisham's novels, a group of preachers schedules a political event at a fundamentalist church. The purpose of the assembly is to rally opposition to a judicial candidate who favors gay rights. Many of the local clergy are invited to participate—but not all of them. In fact, the Methodist ministers in town "were specifically excluded" from taking part in the rally because they were believed to support justice for all persons.[28]

- In one of Mel Brooks's classic films, the satires and parodies are comprehensive and relentless. They address racism, ethnocentrism, sexual obsessions, crass politics, cowardly clergy, corporate corruption, and even the film industry itself. At one point, a crafty government official lists a roster of ruffians that he wants to assemble in an effort to terrorize a town. "I want rustlers, cut throats, murderers, bounty hunters, desperados, mugs, pugs, thugs, nitwits, halfwits, dimwits, vipers, snipers, con men, Indian agents, Mexican bandits, muggers, buggerers, bushwhackers, hornswogglers, horse thieves, . . . and Methodists."[29]

Methodists are visible enough to be characterized, criticized, and caricatured in fiction. But is Methodism really a force that can lead in transforming the world in reality? The answer to that requires clarity about how individuals and organizations lead, how they become leaders, and what leadership means.

In the book on which he was at work at the time of his death, Dr. Edwin Friedman discussed the concept of leadership by self-differentiation. From his experience as a rabbi within a congregation, from his work as a psychologist, and from his consultations with organizations ranging from churches to the military, Friedman concluded that effective leaders must

---

27 CBS Television, *Judging Amy* Season 5, Episode 11, "Christenings," January 6, 2004.

28 John Grisham, *The Appeal* (New York; Doubleday, 2008), 256. References to United Methodism are sprinkled throughout Grisham's many popular novels. See, for example, *Sycamore Row* (New York: Bantam, 2013), 299 and *Gray Mountain* (New York: Dell, 2014), 271.

29 *Blazing Saddles*, screenplay by Mel Brooks et al. (1974 Warner Brothers). The scene, with Harvey Korman and Slim Pickens, can be viewed at https://www.youtube.com /watch?v=fLpmswBKVN4.

understand the complex emotional systems in which communities function. Leadership means having a strong sense of one's own identity, functioning from a sense of one's integrity, maintaining freedom from emotional entanglements formed by others in the community, and distinguishing oneself by the traits of temperament that focus on progress.

Rather than deriving a sense of self from the adulation or the embrace of others, effective leadership depends on knowledge of oneself. So Friedman wanted to "encourage leaders to focus first on their own integrity and on the nature of their own presence rather than through techniques for manipulating or motivating others."[30]

According to Friedman, institutions are "emotional fields,"[31] and effective leaders in organizations or societies are recognized not by "how much power they exercise but how well their *presence* is able to preserve that society's integrity."[32] These leadership principles apply not only to individuals but also to groups. That includes religious organizations. To be recognized and respected as a leader in the world, a church must know its sense of mission, have a strong sense of identity, and demonstrate a clearly differentiated sense of integrity. These are the qualities that characterize effective leaders because these are the qualities that merit respect and earn recognition for leadership.

An effective leader, Friedman says, is a not "peace monger."

> By that I mean a highly anxious risk-avoider, someone who is more concerned with good feelings than with progress, someone whose life revolves around the axis of consensus, a "middler," someone who is so incapable of taking well-defined stands that his "disability" seems to be genetic, someone who functions as if she had been filleted of her backbone.[33]

An effective leader does not surrender self to the emotional systems established by others. Nor does an effective leader colonize or control other persons or communities. Instead, an effective leader has clarity and control of self.

---

30 Edwin Friedman, *A Failure of Nerve: Leadership in the Age of the Quick Fix* (New York: Church Publishing, 2007), 13.

31 Ibid., 15.

32 Ibid., 17 (emphasis added).

33 Ibid., 13.

> I want to stress that by *well-differentiated leader* I do not mean
> an autocrat who tells others what to do or orders them around....
> Rather, I mean someone who has clarity about his or her own life
> goals and, therefore, someone who is less likely to become lost in
> the anxious emotional processes swirling about.[34]

To be specific for religious organizations rather than individuals, a church that is a leader has clarity about its life and its goals. A church that leads is one that will not be anxious about its vitality or stability. A church that leads is one that knows its missional purpose in the world and can articulate how fulfilling its purpose will make a difference in the world. That church can exercise leadership in transforming the world.

Methodism, therefore, can be an effective leader in the world. But Methodism can only lead if it knows itself, if it clearly defines itself, if it strives to be itself, if it clearly articulates its mission, and if it does not get lost in others' emotions. It has led before.

In the past, Methodism was at the front line of educational opportunities, favoring public schools that formed children for citizenship in a democracy, and creating church-related schools, colleges, and universities. The church's mission educated generations of physicians, lawyers, engineers, and teachers. During legalized racial segregation in the nineteenth and twentieth centuries, the church led in establishing "Historically Black Colleges and Universities" (HBCU) to open doors of higher education for those who—by reasons of race alone—were restricted at, or banned from, public and private institutions.

Today, one might look at some of the elite, mostly white universities founded by Methodists and imagine that the letters "UMC" stand for "upper middle class" rather than for The United Methodist Church. Institutions like Northwestern University and Southern Methodist University sit in neighborhoods where the real estate is pricey and where costs of attendance are substantial. Yet these campuses contribute millions of research dollars to improve the social order. They offer millions more in financial aid to students who qualify for admission. They continue the missional purpose for which the church created them—namely, to expand widely the achievements of higher education in research and teaching.

---

34   Ibid., 14 (emphasis added).

They also inspire the founding of similar universities in other lands. Notable today is Africa University, in politically troubled Zimbabwe. It has surpassed a quarter century of achievement on the way to becoming a Pan-Africa institution of higher learning. More are envisioned on other continents to accomplish in mission what American Methodists were determined to accomplish in North America.

In April 1998, on the campus of one of those universities, there was a funeral for Terry Sanford, a United Methodist layperson. In the Chapel of Duke University, where he had been president for sixteen years, his remarkable life of public service was remembered. After serving as special agent with the FBI and as an officer in the United States Army during World War II, he practiced law, and then he entered politics. Following a term as a North Carolina state senator, at age forty-three he was elected to be the state's governor. In an era when its governors could only be elected to one four-year term, he doubled his state's expenditures on public schools, created a community college system, founded a state school of the arts, and advocated desegregation of the public schools.

Among the stories told at his funeral was one from his childhood. When the west campus of Duke University was under construction, thanks to the philanthropy of the Methodist family for whom the university was named, Sanford's parents took him on a trip to see the project. During the visit, Sanford's mother said to him, "We will never be able to afford to send you to school here, but we want you to know that, because we are Methodists, this is our school."

It was a distinguishing mark of mission to be connected to educational ventures for the benefit of the world, including big ventures that went beyond one's individual or personal involvement with them. Methodism was able to differentiate itself by making big commitments to reform the world. Methodism exercised faithful leadership in making education a force for the reformation of the world. Methodism had a mission that could put a poor family from eastern North Carolina in touch with a mystery beyond their best imaginations because it would give them a personal stake in that immense mission. The Sanford family could not send their son as a student to that university, but the family still felt connected to the educational mission of that university. It was just a touch of irony that their son became the leader of a university where he did not attend but where he was known as "Uncle Terry" by thousands of students in the sixteen years that he was their president.

Whatever Methodism becomes—and whatever becomes of Methodism—will be the expression of an identity formed by a sense of mission. Or it will be nothing at all.

A missional identity is not a set of laws about human sexuality or sexual conduct. A missional identity is not an assortment of rules or procedures. A missional identity is not a management strategy for increasing the numbers of members, attendees, assets, or campuses that can be counted. A missional identity is not an assortment of programmatic initiatives to spur dynamic worship or to deploy new technologies. Such things may *serve* the mission of the church. But they are superficial attributes of a sense of identity.

Abraham embraced a call and accepted a mission from God. He had no idea what he would do or where he would go. He simply began a process of discovering the power of a new identity, formed not by tasks but by trust.

When the founders of Methodism embraced their call and accepted their mission to reform the nation and to spread scriptural holiness, they had no idea what that might mean or where it might lead. They simply began a process of letting a new identity shape them and develop them. Convinced that God trusted them, they trusted God and moved toward a horizon as big as the nation, the continent, and the world.

When practitioners of Methodism in the twenty-first century confront our current crises, we have to make decisions that are based on a missional identity—*who*, God trusts, we will become—not on the machinery or the morality of what we think we are.

There are some who would prefer an option that settles for the small things.

- One option is to *do something*. We could call upon our management skills to set numerical goals and train people to achieve them. We could write new church laws and enforce them every time someone breaks a boundary established by the legislation. We could break up the church or break away from the church or loosen our connection to the larger church and thereby seek to cleanse ourselves from all unrighteousness.

- Another option is to *do nothing*, while waiting for the results of persistent and slow decline, a religious revolution, a political disaster, an act of war, an ecological calamity, a financial windfall, or even a return of the

Lord to solve the situation that confronts us. We would not do any harm, basically because we would not do anything at all, except what we are doing out of habit now.

But neither doing something nor doing nothing will deliver us from the doubts and fears that currently confront us.

There is another possibility, however. It draws upon the story of Abraham, who acquired a new identity by faith and who embraced the magnificent mystery of mission. This option is to discover who we are by embracing a sense of mission given to us by God, whom we can trust to provide a differentiating identity that is bigger than any institutional form ever will be or ever will need to be.

When John Wesley said that Methodism's mission was reforming the nation and when the early American Methodists said their mission was reforming the continent, they felt called to participate in mysteries of deliverance for themselves and for the world. They were expressing immense hopes for their tiny organizational structures. Six years after John Wesley convened his first conference of preachers in 1744, the Methodist movement had fewer than forty preachers deployed in England, Ireland, and Wales. In 1750, the Methodists were about 0.1 percent of the population in Great Britain. In London, where Methodism was concentrated, Methodists were about 0.5 percent of the city's population.[35]

Measured by their numbers alone, the early Methodists were making outrageous claims about their place in the world. However, their standard of measurement was the mysterious mission of God. Methodists became a people through a sense of mission that was directed outwardly—to wherever God's children are struggling, suffering, afraid, and dying. Methodism became a people through delivering a message in words and in actions from the Lord to all people. It is still a universal message of death and life.

The Wesleyan theological tradition is in mission to offer a message of deliverance for this age and for the age to come. In theological formulas favored by some Christians, salvation is what comes after one dies. In Wesley's theology, however, salvation "is not a blessing which lies on the other

---

35   Heitzenrater, *Wesley and the People Called Methodists*, 181.

side [of] death . . . it is a present thing . . . the entire work of God, from the first dawning of grace in the soul till it is consummated in glory."[36]

Salvation is a continuous process in this life and in the life to come. It has been cited as a basic element in defining the identity of Methodism by the Committee on Faith and Order that is accountable to the global Council of Bishops in The United Methodist Church.[37] It expresses an ecclesiology, which is a theological understanding of the nature of the church. Titled "Wonder, Love, and Praise," the document offers an answer to the spiritual question about Methodist identity ("Who are we?").

The answer, in short, is that we Methodists are a body of Christians who insist that the message of salvation applies as fully to this life as it does to the life to come. We celebrate the gospel of Jesus Christ as a message of death and life. We offer good news in confronting death, whether that is the biological death that comes to all God's creatures or other forces of death such as the suffering, hunger, injustice, hatred, and slavery that deprive human beings of the freedom for which Christ has set us free. We proclaim the good news that death—in all of its forms—has been overcome by the power of God. In this age and for the age to come, Methodism's mission is to proclaim the good news as a matter of death and life. And we have the theological perspective to do it.

GOING ON TO PERFECTION

One Christian doctrine, that is distinctively—though not exclusively—Wesleyan, teaches a theological principle known as "Christian perfection." Properly understood, it is not a matter of personal morality or ethical infallibility.[38]

Rather, Christian perfection emphasizes a vital aspect of what it means to receive salvation—to be saved and be delivered from sin and death. Christian perfection is being made perfect in love. It is the culmination, completion, and fulfillment of the process of salvation. Moreover, salvation is not merely something to be received. It is to be shared. So it is integral to the

---

36 John Wesley, "The Scripture Way of Salvation," in *The Works of John Wesley: Sermons*, vol. 2, ed. Albert C. Outler (Nashville: Abingdon Press, 1985), 156.

37 "Wonder, Love, and Praise," p. 20.

38 John Wesley, "A Plain Account of Christian Perfection," in *The Works of John Wesley: Doctrinal and Controversial Treatises*, vol. 13, eds. Paul Wesley Chilcote and Kenneth J. Collins (Nashville: Abingdon Press, 2013), 187.

mission of Jesus Christ in the world. Wesley said that perfect love gives us "boldness in the day of judgment, because as he is, so are we in this world."[39]

The goal of salvation is to be made perfect in love in this life. Whether that goal is achievable — or had ever been achieved — is not the point. A Christian seeks to embrace, and to be embraced by, the fullness of God's saving grace. To be a Christian is to pursue perfection, to be filled with grace, and to use love boldly.

Every person seeking clergy membership in a Methodist conference and asking to be ordained as a United Methodist deacon or elder is required to answer in a positive way a set of questions that Wesley devised. The first asks the basic question of Christian faith. The next three draw upon the doctrine of Christian perfection.

1. Have you faith in Christ?

2. Are you going on to perfection?

3. Do you expect to be made perfect in love in this life?

4. Are you earnestly striving after it?[40]

And this doctrine applies to all Methodists, not just to the ministers in the church. In Wesley's view, Christian perfection is to be embraced by everyone. He made it clear that clergy are not just to affirm it. They are to proclaim it and lead people to it. "Therefore, all our preachers should make a point of *preaching perfection* to believers, constantly, strongly, and explicitly. And all believers should 'mind this one thing' and continually agonize for it."[41]

Wesley was widely chastised for his views on Christian perfection. His opponents used it against him. But it was "his distinctive and defining message."[42] And he insisted that it was not narrowly Methodist, as he reminded his critics.

> They wanted, they sought occasion against *me* — and here they found what they sought. "This is Mr. Wesley's doctrine! He preaches perfection!" He does: yet this is not *his* doctrine any more than it is *yours*; or anyone else's that is a minister of Christ.

---

39 Ibid., 163. Wesley cites 1 John 4:18.

40 *The Book of Discipline of The United Methodist Church 2016*, ¶ 336, pp. 270–71.

41 Wesley, "A Plain Account of Christian Perfection," *The Works of John Wesley*, vol. 13, eds. Chilcote and Collins, 188. (The emphasis is his.)

42 Ibid., 134.

> For it is *his* doctrine, peculiarly, emphatically *his*—it is the doctrine of Jesus Christ. Those are *his* words, not mine: "Ye shall therefore be perfect, as your Father who is in heaven is perfect." It is the doctrine of St. Paul, the doctrine of St. James, of St. Peter, and St. John—and no otherwise Mr. Wesley's than as it is the doctrine of everyone who preaches the pure and the whole gospel.[43]

The content of "the whole gospel," as Wesley calls it, is unassailable. "Will anyone dare to speak against loving the Lord our God with all our heart, and our neighbor as ourselves?"[44] So Methodists know who we are. Our mission, which is as big as the nation or the continent or the world, defines us. Our doctrine, to be made perfect in love in this life, teaches us. Our love for God and for our neighbors emboldens us. And our salvation, as a continuous process now and in eternity, delivers us from death into life.

To be saved is to be in the process of deliverance toward becoming perfect in love in this life. To be saved is to be in the midst of living the promise of God. Our mission is fulfilled in the present and focused on the future, with all of its profound uncertainties.

We are bold about our mission because it is based on the perfection to which God is leading us. So the boldness is based on Christian perfection that is driven by a promise, not by moral purity that has been attained. Also, the boldness is derived from a promise given to a community not just to individuals. The promise of God to Abraham centered on a people that would emerge. Similarly, the promise of the Holy Spirit at Pentecost was a gift for the community of faith that was in the midst of coming to be. Individual claims of boldness are based on arrogance or pride rather than perfect love. Wesleyan theology affirms that we are in the process of being saved not solely as individuals but as God's people in a community. And the community is as universal as God's love, in this life and in the life to come. In Wesleyan terms, we have a mission for which we can be bold in connection.

Paul said of Abraham, "No distrust made him waver concerning the promise of God."[45] We are now heirs of that promise. It came to Abraham with an invitation to seek what he had yet to find and to lead a community that had not yet begun. It comes to us in the twenty-first century as a

---

43 Ibid., 189. (The emphasis is his.) The quote from Jesus is in Matthew 5:48.

44 Ibid., 190.

45 Romans 4:20.

summons from God, though our direction may be unfamiliar and our destination may not be where we prefer to go. As disciples of Jesus, we trust God, leading into a future that is filled with murky mysteries.

And they are not only the mysteries that lie beyond the boundary of life on earth. There are also the mysteries that we face during our journey in this lifetime. If we believe salvation is a continuous experience of God's love where life overcomes death, now and in eternity, then we are in the midst of the same saving process on this side of the grave as we will be on the other side.

Going on to perfection is a matter of death and life. Our mission is to proclaim in bold ways that God's grace is saving us continuously, in this life and in the life to come. Death is the last enemy.[46] It has many weapons. We must confront it wherever and whenever we face it. Sometimes, we wish we did not have to do that.

A prominent pastor in one United Methodist annual conference was very pleased when he and his wife heard from both of their young adult sons that they felt called into the ordained ministry. Not long thereafter, both young men began theological studies as candidates for ordination. After his first year, one of the sons told his parents that it was important for the three of them to have a conversation. The young man said to his mother and father that he had come to accept his identity as a gay man and that even though he still felt clearly called to pastoral ministry he knew that the law of The United Methodist Church would prevent him from fulfilling his call within the denomination.

The father told a congregation that the news left him perplexed and conflicted and hurt. It was at odds with his moral views about homosexuality. It tormented his affection for his son. And it tore at his relationship with the denomination, whose *Discipline* he was determined to honor. One of his actions in response to this situation was to begin a discipline of daily devotion and prayer. Every day, he said, he prayed the same prayer: "Lord, either change my son or change me."

He did not know how long into the future that pattern of prayer would endure, nor did he know what the answer to that prayer might be. Indeed, he did not know whether the prayer would yield any answer at all. As it

---

46   1 Corinthians 15:26.

happened, he explained, his daily prayer continued for a year: "Lord, either change my son or change me." At the end of the year, the answer came. The father said, "God changed me."

By the grace of God, he experienced a transformation of perspective on moral judgments and on the ecclesiastical laws of the denomination. It was a gift of deliverance. It was one step in the process of going on to perfection, of being made perfect in love in this life. And it brought reconciliation to father and son.

It also provoked a problem within the church. The bishop moved the father to a new pastoral appointment because conflicts arose in the charge. Some church members doubted whether it was appropriate for the father to be so open about his love for his gay son. Others wondered how anyone, even a parent, could love a homosexual person.

What is perfect love? How is it manifest in mission? How is it to be preached in pulpits? How is it to be displayed by disciples? How can it be pursued unless it is being practiced? How can we be saved without insisting on it? How can we be delivered from death without living within the power that defeats death? How can we know the freedom of deliverance without knowing the truth that sets us free? How can such a theological idea come to life as an institution? How can we build a church on it?

In the twenty-eighth chapter of Isaiah, the prophet of the Lord describes an encounter where God confronts powerful "scoffers" who distrust the promises of God. According to the prophet, the scoffers' position is, "We have made a covenant with death . . . for we have made lies our refuge, and in falsehood we have taken shelter."[47] The Lord responds by promising to build a new structure—not a "shelter" based on "lies" but a sanctuary with "a sure foundation" and a "precious cornerstone" that is inscribed with the words, "One who trusts will not panic." The standards for the structure will be aligned with "justice" and "righteousness." And, in the process, says the Lord to the scoffers by way of the prophet, "Then your covenant with death will be annulled."[48]

The forces of death are constructed out of lies, falsehoods, and panic. The forces of life are constructed out of justice, righteousness, and boldness.

47   Isaiah 28:15.

48   Isaiah 28:14–18.

Going on to perfection, in matters of death and life, is trusting God and living within a structure of justice, righteousness, and boldness.

In the crisis that is currently confronting The United Methodist Church, the word of the Lord that came through the prophet Isaiah should be engraved on the cornerstone of our connectional system: "One who trusts will not panic." We do not need to euthanize the church. We do not need to ensmall it within congregations or conferences or contexts that suit our comforts. Instead, we need boldly to engage in a mission that is broader than our eyes can see or bigger than our calculations can count.

Without doubt, Methodism in general and United Methodism in particular are in the midst of great anxieties. And yet, even in a moment of crisis, the cornerstone of our structure is what Isaiah said in the name of the Lord: "One who trusts will not panic."

So Methodism need not panic on the path to being made perfect in love in life. Its local and connectional systems provide a platform for hope. This does not mean that each element in the system must be protected and preserved. Some local churches will die. So will some agencies, offices, and rules. But the bold mission of connectional Methodism must be to bring life to the communities where congregations close. The death of a local church cannot mean that the gospel goes silent where people still suffer injustice, endure unrighteousness, and remain in the prisons of all sorts of addictions—including greed and pride.

TOWARD A BOLD GLOBAL MISSION

The United Methodist Church today likes to describe itself as a global church. It certainly can do so since there is a United Methodist presence on every continent except Antarctica. Also, its global nature is not only in terms of its geographical expanse. It has become global through time as well. From the days of John Wesley, through big missionary endeavors, evangelization, social transformation, and institutional expansion, the global character of the church flourished into World Methodism.

The late Bishop James K. Mathews often noted that the General Conference of The United Methodist Church is the largest, most representative, democratic legislative body in the longest continuous service in the world. But, for now, this global body has limited itself with a local sense of mission. And many tensions are straining the multiple threads of the web that holds global United Methodism together. So the notion of worldwide Methodism that functions in many places in a global connection may exceed the capacity of even the most imaginative believers among us.

Yet such a Methodist presence is not a phantom or a figment of imagination. It is a reality. What it lacks is a shared sense of mission.

For example, in West Africa, Methodism in the nation of Nigeria is in disarray. In part, that is because there are Methodists and there are United Methodists in Nigeria. The United Methodist Church has one bishop who oversees four annual conferences within the country. Based on the size of its allocated General Conference delegation, the Southern Nigeria Annual Conference alone is as large as the Baltimore-Washington Conference in the United States. And that is only one of four annual conferences in the country. Meanwhile, The Methodist Church in Nigeria has fifty-four bishops, and it has an undetermined number of members. Amid these uncertainties, some United Methodists in the United States affirm—and financially support—the Methodist Church in Nigeria, possibly without any awareness that there is no known accountability system in place for the financial contributions they provide.

The comprehensive Methodist mission in Nigeria is distressed. The condition of Methodism, including United Methodism, in Nigeria continues in disarray. Besides these ecclesial difficulties, the country itself is facing dismaying difficulties. Northern Nigeria is home to Boko Haram, the terrorist group that adheres to a twisted interpretation of Islam. Boko Haram disallows any form of Western education, kidnaps boys to turn them into bearers of military weapons (often "weaponizing" the boys themselves), and kidnaps girls to turn them into sexual servants of their soldiers.

The United States has in recent years supported efforts to achieve some kind of stability in northern Nigeria. However, the administration in Washington since January 20, 2017, has vowed to eliminate that aid.

Just over the northern border of Nigeria is the nation of Niger. Most of its people are concentrated in southern Niger, near the border with Nigeria, because 80 percent of the land in Niger is the Sahara Desert. It appears that only two things are growing in Niger. One is the desert itself, by a process of "desertification" of the land. The other is population. John Micklethwait, the editor in chief of *Bloomberg*, says the prospects are terrifying. "In Niger, climate change is wrecking crops even as technology is helping more children survive, so a population of 19 million will reach 72 million hungry people by 2050."[49]

The local churches in United Methodism have no capacity to address this. And the Methodists along with the United Methodists in Nigeria lack the resources to confront it.

Doing nothing seems scarcely to be an option, unless Methodists are willing to watch millions of people die by starvation. Doing something seems wise, unless it is the wrong thing or a totally insufficient and misguided thing.

Only a massive, mysterious missional identity can inspire and enable the twenty-first century followers of John Wesley to find a way to reform the continent in West Africa. Only forceful, faithful political action by Methodists including United Methodists in the United States could alter the policy of the American government and restore stabilizing aid to northern Nigeria and Niger.

It will take boldness that is borne of love on its way to perfection, if the church in the world is to bring deliverance from death to life in that part of Africa.[50] It will take boldness that draws upon the spirit of Wesley's conference in Bristol in 1745, when the Methodists said, "National sins call aloud for national judgments."[51]

Other situations face other Methodists in other parts of the world. The mission is big and bold enough for a creative Wesleyan witness.

In southern Asia, Methodism in Malaysia has a widespread presence. Six annual conferences have ministries that are organized primarily around ethnicity, language, and culture. Less than a tenth of Malaysia's thirty-one million people are Christians, and of the Christians only about two hundred thousand are Methodists. Hence, in this majority Muslim country, Methodists are a tiny minority—far less than 1 percent of the population. Yet they have an identity and a vibrancy evident in their worship, in their commitment to education, in their determination to have a well-trained cadre of pastoral leaders, and in their courage as they address the challenges of being

---

49 John Micklethwait, review of *Thank You for Being Late: An Optimist's Guide to Thriving in the Age of Accelerations*, by Thomas L. Friedman, *New York Times Book Review*, December 18, 2016.

50 Wesley, "A Plain Account of Christian Perfection," *The Works of Wesley*, vol. 13, ed. Chilcote and Collins, 187; 1 John 4:17.

51 "The Bristol Conference of August 1–3, 1745," *The Works of John Wesley: The Methodist Societies, The Minutes of Conference*, vol. 10, ed. Rack, 158.

Christian in a country that tolerates multiple religions but tests the limits of that toleration from time to time.

One recent test involved the text of the Bible in the languages of ethnic groups in the country. Most Malaysians are fluent in at least two languages and function in three or more. The Malay people are the largest ethnic group, and their language is predominant.

Scriptures translated into Malay have long used the word "Allah" as the name for God. However, political tensions and persecutions have ensnared Christians, including Methodists, over the use of that word. One Methodist conference embraces an indigenous people who are known as Iban. Their language has only one word for God, namely Allah. The Iban Methodists can read about, and pray to, "Allah" in their own tongue. But if other Methodists in Malaysia, who read biblical texts or pray or preach in Malay, use the word "Allah," they can face repercussions.

For Methodists who live in nations where Christianity is the religion either of the majority or of a substantial minority, such troubles are unfathomable. United Methodists in the United States who fall victim to fears about the influence of non-Christian religions need to adopt a global perspective when we are going on to perfection. The Methodists in Malaysia have much to teach United Methodists in North America about what it means to love those who might try to restrict religious liberties and what it means to engage in evangelism where proselytizing for religious purposes is forbidden by law.

Moreover, United Methodists could learn a lot about the mission of the church by listening to Christians elsewhere in Asia. In Hong Kong, for example, missional identity requires three kinds of activity before a community can actually be declared a "church": it must gather as a community for worship; it must be engaged in education; and it must be active in at least one form of direct social outreach to the people in the vicinity. This is a balanced portfolio for mission. Unless all three elements are present in mission, the community simply does not qualify as "church" in that Asian context.

These are examples from Africa and Asia. United Methodists could also benefit from other Methodists' experience in the southern hemisphere.

In all of Latin America, only Honduras has "United" Methodism. In other areas, from Cuba in the Caribbean to the southern tips of Argentina and Chile, autonomous and independent Methodists are the Wesleyan presence. The Methodist Church of Peru (*Iglesia Methodista del Perú*) is one of them.

Methodists in Peru are not members of The United Methodist Church.

They are an autonomous church in the global community of World Methodism. However, Methodists in Peru value their relationship with The United Methodist Church. For example, they have borrowed and adapted some United Methodist symbols for their own use. The logo for *Iglesia Methodista del Perú* is a map of the country with a "Cross and Flame" (the emblem of The United Methodist Church) superimposed on an outline map of the nation. The symbol for the *obispo* (bishop) of Peruvian Methodism closely resembles the symbol for the United Methodist bishops.

The lay leader of the Methodists in Peru has retired from a professional career in international business and is now leading the church in creating institutions for education—at the primary, secondary, and collegiate levels. He works closely with the bishop on these matters. So the leadership of the church has a strong sense of connectional identity with Peruvian culture and commerce, with Wesleyan theology and practice, and with a big missional commitment.

Yet North American United Methodists would find the Methodist presence in Peru to be quite different from their experience. Only about one-tenth of 1 percent of the population in Peru is Methodist. And a sizable percentage of Peruvian Methodists live at the low end of the social and economic scale.

Those are not the only noticeable differences. Sunday morning worship often occurs in small storefronts on urban streets. What happens in the context of worship is a combination of study, prayer, and social outreach. Bible classes for all ages meet prior to worship, and then each class must stand in front of the congregation during worship to recite the Bible passages they learned in class. Social outreach occurs in the context of worship, as food and household goods are gathered for those in need, and the recipients accept their baskets and bundles during worship.

In addition, church life in the "suburbs" of big cities does not mean sprawling campuses with comfortable buildings. The norm, instead, is dirt floors and no running water.

There is a suburb of the capital city, Lima, known as *Lomas de Carabayllo*. It is one of the poorest areas in Peru. The region is a dusty hillside, with roughly built homes along dirt streets and walkways. Since there is no public utility system for the residents, water arrives by truck on a regular basis and is stored in large vats or tanks on site. Along an unpaved street in the community is a structure with the logo of the church—an outline of Peru with a cross and flame superimposed on it—above the entrance.

Ready to greet any visitor is a woman whose family resides on the premises. She serves as a combination of custodian, deacon, sexton, verger, and trustee for the church. The portion of the property that is used for worship has a dirt floor and no roof. So one of her tasks on Sundays is to take some precious water from the storage tank and sprinkle it on the dirt floor, to keep the dust settled. She moves a Communion table and lectern into sanctuary space. Then worshipers gather. The moistened floor minimizes the dust when the church dances during the service.

Below the hillside in *Lomas de Carabayllo* are verdant agricultural fields where many of the residents do manual labor and earn the meager incomes that sustain them. On the upper stretches of the hillside are the homes where they reside, with the same kinds of dirt floors that are beneath their feet at worship, and where small groups meet for prayer or Bible study as extended families during the week. Visitors are always welcome. But as a visitor, one must be prepared to offer and accept prayer. It is astonishing how bold the people of faith can be in their mission to share the process of being made perfect in love in this life.

One might think that such people called Methodist practice their piety in isolation from global Methodism and pursue their path to Christian perfection in their own private ways. Actually, they feel connected to the wider community of Methodists. The church's lay leader is a native Peruvian whose family had come to Peru from Japan. He spent part of his business career in his home country and part of it in the country of his ancestors. In a conversation one day, I told him that one of my pastoral appointments was in a rather small town in Pennsylvania. I mentioned that two of the members were sisters, both of whom had served as Methodist missionaries—one in Peru and the other in Japan. I told him their names. He replied, "I knew them both." He had met the younger sister in Japan, where she did missionary work with children. And he had met the older sister in Peru through his involvements in Peruvian Methodist life.

There are many dimensions to the distinctively Wesleyan theological principle of going on to perfection and being made perfect in love in this life. We can all grow in our knowledge of and respect for the amazing diversity of the peoples called Methodist who are living the good news of life that overcomes so many forms of death. The mysterious mission to which God invites us is a confrontation not only with physical death but also with suffering, injustice, poverty, loneliness, bias, prejudice, and political powers that are cruelly indifferent to God's children. Wherever the Methodist mission lives, the rest of us have much to learn from those who are practicing the faith in the face of challenges that may be unfamiliar to—and unfathomable by—those of us in different circumstances.

The doctrine of Christian perfection is not only something important for United Methodists to teach but also something important for United Methodists to learn. It is vital to our salvation that we are made perfect in love in this life with global Methodism, with non-Christian religious people including the Abrahamic peoples, namely Muslims and Jews, as well as adherents of other religious systems.

United Methodists in America, for instance, have our own challenges that must be faced. Many have too long been accustomed to places of economic privilege in the social order and to the ranks of religious privilege that we have under Americans' constitutional order. We have given too little attention to the journey toward Christian perfection when it involves people of all ethnicities, economic classes, political persuasions, and religious affiliations. We have been too silent when Muslims, Jews, and adherents of other faiths have been vilified. We have been too ensmalled into congregational life when the mission to which we have been called beckons us to bigger mysteries. We have been starstruck by the size of big congregations when we should also have been seeking to saturate our communities and countries and continents with the power of the connection.

When a local church dies or is institutionally helped to die, we must do more than mourn and remember. When a denomination threatens to divide or dissolve, we must do more than choose the side that affirms our perspective.

There are many vacant spaces that must be filled by the Methodist mission, which has a mysterious gift of life to offer in those places. There are educational initiatives that need to be launched. There are substance abusers and addicts that need the good news of liberation. There are estrangements based on race that need to be reconciled. There are political oppressors whose grip needs to be loosened There are victims of violence that need to taste victory. There are hungry who need to be fed. There are desperate ones who need deliverance from despair. There are dying ones who need hope—for this life and for the life to come. And all of these situations are out there in the miraculous mission field to which God is inviting us and sending us. If we trust the Lord, we need not panic.

The God who called Abraham and who sent Jesus has promises to keep that will not be honored by the petty politics of polity. We need a boldness that knows no bounds! We are going on to perfection in this life. And, as the last chorus of Requiem says, we trust God's grace to guide us to the promise of paradise.

QUESTIONS FOR DISCUSSION

1. How does the mission of the church relate to other religions and traditions?

   • Islam?

   • Judaism?

   • Latter Day Saints?

   • Roman Catholics?

   • Eastern Orthodox?

2. Should a church have a mission statement that is concise, memorable, and repeatable?

3. What matters more in the mission of the church, the connection or the congregation?

4. Are you going on to perfection?

   • Do you expect to be made perfect in love in this life?

   • Are you earnestly striving after it?

5. Can one be made perfect in love and still hate another person or group?

6. What will it mean for the church to move from a majority to a minority status?

EPILOGUE

BEARING THE PROMISE OF PARADISE

The Anglican parish at Epworth, where Susannah and Samuel Wesley lived and raised their many children while Samuel was the parish priest, has a graveyard on the church grounds. One of the gravesites is the resting place of Samuel, where John Wesley boldly stood and boldly preached when his father's successor refused to let the upstart founder of Methodism deliver a sermon inside the church's walls.

But another gravesite also deserves to be noticed. It is the resting place of a man named Thomas Cutforth, who had been arrested in 1720 in Epworth for stealing. Local authorities convicted him of the theft, hanged him for his crime, and left his body hanging in the Market Square apparently as a message to deter anyone else from such criminal conduct.

Samuel Wesley, who was still the rector at the time, could not abide the practice of letting death dominate the life of the village. He took the body of Mr. Cutforth down and conducted a proper Christian burial in the parish cemetery. He was not ignorant of the man's crime. But he was determined that the witness of the church focus on hope rather than humiliation, on love rather than law, on life rather than death.

So on March 27, 1720, Samuel Wesley presided at a Christian funeral for a man who had broken the law and who had then been victimized by the legal system. A plaque on the gravesite, which recounts the episode, has an epitaph that Samuel Wesley wrote. It concludes, "Thomas Cutforth, I hope, is gone to rest."

> May the angels lead you into paradise;
> May the martyrs receive you at your arrival
> And lead you to the holy city Jerusalem.
> May choirs of angels receive you
> And with Lazarus, once a poor man,
> May you have eternal rest.

In Paradisum (Into Paradise) from Requiem

CPSIA information can be obtained
at www.ICGtesting.com
Printed in the USA
LVOW11s1415060418
572569LV00004B/180/P